Dr. Robert Ballard

Understanding Levels Of

STRATEGIC
SPIRITUAL
WARFARE

It will make all the difference

Strategic Spiritual Warfare

Published by
Maurice Wylie Media
Bethel Media House
Tobermore
Magherafelt,
Northern Ireland
BT45 5SG (UK)

Publisher's Statement: *Throughout this book, the love for our God is such that whenever we refer to Him, we illustrate our honor to Him by capitalization of all references. On the other hand, we will violate the rules of grammar by withholding capitalization of all references to the devil, as we refuse to acknowledge him with any honor.*

For more information visit
www.MauriceWylieMedia.com

Contents

Foreword

I have known the author of Strategic Spiritual Warfare, Dr. Robert Ballard, as a great preacher and teacher of the Gospel. His previous career engagements in the US Army, gives him the necessary tools and experience to deal with the subject of this book. He has tactically, with eloquence, used military terms to excavate the Gospel truth, to provide his readers with vital ammunitions to wage spiritual war against the devil.

This masterpiece is a perfect Christian discourse in dealing with strategic spiritual warfare, the finest I have ever read. Dr. Robert Ballard proves mastery in his analysis and translation of military strategic planning systems in a war situation, to the spiritual war that Christians encounter with the devil and his demons. The spiritual world is intertwined with complexities that are difficult to delve into, but the author manages to get into spiritual depth, to bring out and illustrate effectively, those proper and successful strategies required to engage in spiritual warfare.

The author has indeed deliberated on areas that some contemporary preachers, teachers, and Christians in general, have seriously erred, marking the doctrinal errors and heresies of our age. Mostly, people focus on the devil and his evil machinations against children of God, instead of focusing on Jesus Christ and His resurrection power. We need to magnify Christ, for the battle is not ours, but God's. (2 Chronicles 20:15)

6

Christians need to know that a strategy is a well-planned action, intended or designed to render the enemy incapable of making war. The author categorically states that in order to accomplish the mission, we need "to pray, proclaim the Word, carry the cross, use spiritual gifts, work in unity, participate in sacraments and live in righteousness, the Holy Spirit responds and wages the warfare to bring glory to Jesus Christ and victory to the Kingdom of Heaven."

The Bible expresses vividly that since time immemorial, the battle line has been drawn between the Kingdom of God and that of the devil. The devil has always tried to destroy the Kingdom of God, but to no avail. God's people should know and believe that they have access to the best spiritual weapons available, to use against the "accuser of brethren." It has been said, "that in every war, there are battles, in every battle, there are attacks." As Christians, we experience these attacks in varying degrees. Some attacks seem like skirmishes, some like never ending battles, and some battles seem like all out fully fledged war. The more that we learn the truths concerning spiritual warfare, the more prepared we can be to fight, and to be righteously victorious.

Dr. Robert Ballard, in this excellent book, prescribes the weapons required for spiritual warfare, and he has determinedly gone out to demonstrate how, if we are obedient to God, we can win the war before we even get into the battlefield. There is nothing that terrifies the devil more than a Christian who is strategically positioned in the Word of God, and one who remains focused on Jesus Christ.

This book gives us all we need to be powerful soldiers of Christ. Dr. Robert Ballard has brought to our disposal, a strategic training manual to equip Christians in their essential spiritual warfare.

Bishop Phillip Tapiwa Walter Mpindu,
The Methodist Revival Church, Harare

Spiritual warfare is not something you can opt into when you feel you're up for it, and neither is it something you can opt out of. The fact is, each of us are already participants, as Paul said "Our struggle is... against the rulers, against the authorities, against the powers of this dark world and against the spiritual forces of evil in the Heavenly realms." (Ephesians 6.12) Robert Ballard addresses this struggle as he takes us on a journey of spiritual warfare.

Robert and I have several things in common. We both left the military in 1977 to follow our pursuit of God's will for our lives. I left the Ulster Defence Regiment in Northern Ireland to attend Bible College in England, while Robert left the US Military to attend seminary in the USA. Several years later our paths were destined to come together in ministry within Northern Ireland.

The second thing we have in common is that both of us are where we are today not only because of God's call on our lives, but because each of us had an older saint of God praying for us.

The third thing we have in common is our love for Jesus Christ and for the lost, which is something that is so evident in this book, a book that details Robert's pursuit of the call of God on his life, a life that has taken him across the USA into prisons and churches, and around the world to places like Armenia, North Korea, China, and of course Belfast, where we first connected, and where we joined together in carrying a cross through the divided streets of the city, an event written about by Robert when he refers to the cross as a weapon to be used in our spiritual warfare.

As you go through this journey you will see that spiritual warfare is not something you simply win on your knees, but it is won on your feet in the battlefields of life. I am therefore delighted to recommend *Strategic Spiritual Warfare* as a book not only worth reading, but worth having in your spiritual armoury.

Pastor Jack McKee, New Life Church, Belfast

Introduction

I will never forget a day back in December 1977. I had completed my four years of military service with the United States Army the month before, and was about to begin my studies at seminary in January. In the interim, I had the opportunity to return to my hometown to visit with family and friends, over the Christmas holidays. One friend, Charlie Webb asked me if I had stopped in to see "Mom" Ellis.

"Mom" and "Pop" Ellis were my neighbors when I was a small child. They were very elderly (my thinking here is that she was very old when I was a young child and since I was almost 30, I felt that she had certainly died by now) so I had no reason to believe that she would even be alive. She had kept me when my parents were away, and often I would go to their house just to have fun. I remember how I would enjoy sitting on their front porch, and play silly games with them and their grandchildren, who would sometimes visit from out of town.

Charlie told me that she was indeed still alive, but she was now blind, and she was living in a nursing home nearby.

I decided to go and visit her and when I knocked on her door, it startled her. I opened the door and found a tiny room with only a bed, a chair and a dresser. When she asked who I was and I told her; she screamed with excitement, grabbed my hand, and told me to sit down. Before I could say anything to her, she proceeded to tell me something that would make an everlasting impact on me.

She said, "The Lord showed me, when you were three years old, you would become a preacher. He also told me to pray for you every day. For the past 23 years, I have been praying for you, each day. I prayed that you would become a Christian. I prayed that He would protect you. I prayed that He would prepare you for ministry. I prayed that you would fall so deeply in love with Jesus nothing in this world would prevent you from serving Him."

Then she looked me straight in the eye and asked, "What are you doing with your life?"

In my stunned condition, I could only reply, "Well, I have surrendered my life to preach, and I begin seminary next month."

After our very pleasant visit and many times since, I have pondered the fact that "Mom" had prayed for me. She prayed for me every day while I was lost without Christ. She prayed for me every day when I would argue that there was no God. She prayed for me every day when I was looking for meaning in life apart from Jesus. Even though she did not know that I had become a Christian, she continued to pray for me every day after I gave my life to Jesus.

She prayed for me each day that I was in the Army. I had thought that I had made my own decision to attend the chapel services at Cooke Barracks in Germany. Now I think that the Lord was leading me there in response to her prayers.

When I was at Ft. Pickett, Virginia, she prayed for me when I was looking for a good congregation, and a great pastor, Bob Gibson, to help me get involved in ministry; and Bob is still my friend to this day. Because of St. Marks United Methodist Church, I was able to learn about, apply to, and be accepted for, a seminary.

Then I got to thinking about all the times that I had thought I was doing some great things for Jesus. In my pride, I had felt that I was dynamic in my personal evangelism. I had led many people to Christ. I was confident in my public speaking, teaching, and preaching. But…

After my meeting with "Mom" Ellis, I sincerely believe, if I have earned any precious stones or any crowns in Heaven, Jesus will take those precious stones and crowns, and place them on her head.

I have also pondered the fact that for many years; her prayers did not appear to make any difference in the times when I was in total rebellion against Jesus Christ and the Kingdom of Heaven; yet, she prayed. I had total disregard to the ways of the Lord; meanwhile, "Mom" was praying for me. I was even vocal and disrespectful in my opposition to Jesus; yet, she was praying every day!

While I was not making positive changes, and was living for the devil, she was telling the forces of darkness, for 23 years, that they could not have me.

What was she doing? She was declaring in the Heavenly realm that Jesus had a purpose for my life. "Mom" Ellis was involved in strategic spiritual warfare. The question is: Have you entered warfare to see your family and loved ones freed, for surely someone did it for you! If you haven't, maybe it is time you did and this book will help you do just that!

Kingdom Warriors

Almost every nation in the world began with some type of war. For instance; in the United States, children study the Revolutionary war with England, from grade school. England had many wars and battles in her history of over 1000 years. France was rocked by a revolution which continued for many years before stability and security was re-established for the people. The Soviet Union began with a revolution against the Czar. While fighting the Japanese in the days of World War II, China was also fighting a civil war with followers of the Communist Mao and Chiang Kai-Shek who sought control. Within hours of the United Nations establishing the nation of Israel in 1948, many of her Arab neighbors attacked. Israel had to fight to keep her independence. Even Joshua in Biblical times took the Promised Land with military conquest.

The Kingdom of God is no different from any other kingdom. It too will be established by warfare. Jesus promised *'You will be hearing of wars and rumors of wars.'* (Matthew 24:6) He also said the *'Kingdom of heaven suffers violence.'* (Matthew 11:12) Therefore, we as Christians must be prepared for battle.

Of course, the battle we face is not against flesh and blood. (Ephesians 6:12) A flesh and blood battle would be easier as we could see the enemy and enter into battle resulting in their destruction. However, even though our battle is against the unseen spiritual forces of wickedness, it is just as real and destructive.

In revolutions, and in other wars which have occurred in our world over the past centuries, there have been not only front line warriors but also those behind the scenes fighting strategically for their cause. This book is an examination of their strategic work, and a look at how we need to be involved strategically in our battle against the forces of hell, who are fighting with cunning and determination to destroy you and me. Therefore, we must be wise, and learn to depend on the Holy Spirit for constant guidance, in order to know how to win this battle as Kingdom warriors.

CHAPTER 1

What is Spiritual Warfare?

Two foundational passages on spiritual warfare are found in Ephesians 6 and 2 Corinthians 10.

'Finally, be strong in the Lord and in the strength of His might. Put on the full armor of God, so that you will be able to stand firm against the schemes of the devil. For our struggle is not against flesh and blood, but against the rulers, against the powers, against the world forces of this darkness, against the spiritual forces of wickedness in the heavenly places. Therefore, take up the full armor of God, so that you will be able to resist in the evil day, and having done everything, to stand firm. Stand firm therefore, having girded your loins with truth, and having put on the breastplate of righteousness, and having shod your feet with the preparation of the Gospel of peace; in addition to all, taking up the shield of faith with which you will be able to extinguish all the flaming arrows of the evil one. And take the helmet of salvation, and the sword of the Spirit, which is the word of God. With all prayer and petition pray at all times in the Spirit, and with this in view, be on the alert with all perseverance and petition for all the saints.' Ephesians 6:10-18

*'For though we walk in the flesh, we do not war according to the flesh, for the weapons of our warfare are not of the flesh, but **divinely powerful** for the destruction of fortresses. We are destroying speculations and every lofty thing raised up against the knowledge*

of God, and we are taking every thought captive to the obedience of Christ.' 2 Corinthians 10:3-5

The term "divinely powerful" in verse 4 should give us much encouragement as we enter into spiritual warfare. The weapons we have from the Lord are more powerful than we can ever understand. We mere mortal, weak and ignorant human beings can never fully comprehend the power of Jesus Christ, nor the power of the weapons He has given us to engage the forces of darkness for His glory, except through the Holy Spirit.

In this book, I want to explain to you the weapons which are at our disposal, as we march forward in Jesus. We can confidently be all we should be in the Lord with these weapons. Of course, we need to use them as they are intended. For instance; we can carry our Bibles; however, if we do not study the Bible, proclaim the Bible, and live according to the direction of the Bible, then we are not using the weapons correctly, which Jesus has given to us. We can sing songs and listen to sermons, but if our spirits are not filled with the Holy Spirit, and if we fail to focus on Jesus, then we will not shake hell with our worship.

Paul writes above in 2 Corinthians 10:5 *'we are taking every thought captive to the obedience of Christ.'* He means that the spiritual battlefield is our mind, and therefore it is of vital importance to be focused on Jesus.

It is so easy for our mind to stray and even to dwell on sinful, lustful, and worldly thoughts. I once heard when the devil sees a Christian on his knees, the devil does not run in fear; instead he gets down next to the Christian and tries his best to distract him. Are you being distracted?

Let me be upfront here. Engaging in spiritual warfare is not for the timid or the weak. But the Bible does state, *'Let the weak say, 'I am strong.'* (Joel 3:10 NKJV) In addition of course, we must remember in our flesh that we are all timid and weak. Therefore, since we must rely on the power of the Holy Spirit to do the fighting, it is thus necessary for each Christian to seek empowerment from the Holy Spirit, to stay focused on Jesus.

When James wrote James 4:7, *'Submit therefore to God. Resist the devil and he will flee from you.'* He was stressing the fact that victorious spiritual warfare requires action on our part, and He did not mean - attend church!

The Christian must be engaged in resisting the devil, or he will not flee. All too often, too many Christians and congregations would prefer to ignore the devil; they seem to have the attitude, "If we do not bother him then he will not bother us." They fail to understand, of course, that if a Christian or a congregation is not going to resist, then they will not be useful for the Kingdom of Heaven; as a result, the devil has no reason to get involved. By their failure to resist, those people or groups have become impotent for the Kingdom, and darkness can prevail. Let us get honest: there is too much darkness in our communities, and sometimes in our families, even in churches. The only way to eliminate it is through you, the believer, the Christian, the Church, the instrument ordained by Jesus to bring light. Jesus told us, *'You are the light of the world.'* Matthew 5:14

A powerful passage in Revelation 12 stresses the omnipotence of Christ in this spiritual battle:

'Then I heard a loud voice in heaven, saying, 'Now the salvation, and the power, and the Kingdom of our God and the authority of His Christ have come, for the accuser of our brethren has been thrown down, he who accuses them before our God day and night. And they overcame him because of the blood of the Lamb and because of the word of their testimony, and they did not love their life even when faced with death.' Revelation 12:10-11

Warfare of any kind on any level requires sacrifice by everyone involved. The idea of an enemy so committed to his cause, willing to joyfully and knowingly kill themselves in an attempt to kill you, is very sobering. Think about this: Moslem suicide bombers are willing to lay down their lives for a lie, why cannot Christians live their lives with abandon for the truth? If we love Jesus more than we love our own lives, our determination becomes a weapon that no demon can overcome.

In the cold war days, when it was said, Soviet soldiers declared themselves to be "dead men on furlough," they were demonstrating their desire to lose their lives by whatever means necessary, to further the cause of communism.

If Moslem suicide bombers and Soviet soldiers dedicated themselves totally to warfare, should not Christians be willing to risk everything as well?

Am I advocating suicide missions for Jesus? No! However, the sobering truth is that we should be willing to risk everything when entering spiritual warfare, especially since we are armed with weapons that no force of hell can overcome.

In John 8:44, Jesus teaches that the devil is a liar, and the father of lies. Therefore, the truth which is the Word of God is a weapon against him. Jesus said, '*I am the way, and the truth, and the life*' John 14:6. We must not only have a relationship with Jesus, and study the Bible, but we must also use those Scriptures which declare the Truth, not only to the world, but into the Heavenly places as well. We can and should remind the devil that he is a defeated foe. As Scripture states, '*Greater is He who is in you than he who is in the world*,' (1 John 4:4) and '*through death He (Jesus) might render powerless him who had the power of death, that is, the devil*.' (Hebrews 2:14)

The Church, you and I, need to see how powerless the forces of darkness really are. The devil is more noise than anything else which reminds me of the scene in the *Wizard of Oz* movie. Dorothy, Scarecrow, Tin Man and the Lion, are standing in front of this huge screen bellowing smoke and flashing lights. A booming voice is creating fear in their hearts, and as their bodies shake in fear, Toto, the little dog, goes around to a curtain and pulls it back.

Suddenly, a little man is exposed shouting into a microphone while pulling wheels and pushing buttons. Dorothy runs over and asks, "Who are you?" He exclaims in a deep voice, "I am the great and ..." then meekly continues, "Powerful wizard of Oz." The devil, like this wizard, has no power except to intimidate; except to create fear; except to bring confusion in those who are living in ignorance to his true identity and impotence. The only power the devil really has is the power that a human being gives him, overtly or covertly.

Jesus gave Paul a mission, described in Acts.

'And I said, 'Who are You, Lord?' And the Lord said, 'I am Jesus whom you are persecuting. But get up and stand on your feet; for this purpose I have appeared to you, to appoint you a minister and a witness not only to the things which you have seen, but also to the things in which I will appear to you; rescuing you from the Jewish people and from the Gentiles, to whom I am sending you, to open their eyes so that they may turn from darkness to light and from the dominion of Satan to God, that they may receive forgiveness of sins and an inheritance among those who have been sanctified by faith in Me.' Acts 26:15-18

This passage makes clear that Paul's mission was spiritual warfare, and the Church today should embrace this same mission of turning people from darkness to light, and from the dominion of satan to God.

Another two passages which shed light on spiritual warfare are 1 John 3:8 and John 10:10 respectively:

'The Son of God appeared for this purpose, to destroy the works of the devil.' 1 John 3:8

'The thief comes only to steal and kill and destroy; I came that they may have life, and have it abundantly.' John 10:10

Both passages tell us that spiritual warfare means destruction. Jesus came to destroy the works of the devil, and the devil is a thief who seeks to destroy our lives. As Jesus is allowed to be Lord, the Holy Spirit will grant a quality of life which the Scriptures describe as "Abundant Life."

Three Errors in Spiritual Warfare

1. Many Christians do not have enough involvement or interest in spiritual warfare. They ignore it or try to stay out of it. There is a lack of understanding and appreciation that every believer is a soldier for Christ. I cannot over estimate this enough - **We do not have a choice to be in battle. Our choice is whether we fight and how we fight.**

Some Christians see spiritual warfare as something for those "called" to it. They may say, "That is wonderful for you but I am called to children's ministry." Their failure to be involved in spiritual warfare will result in their children's ministry not achieving everything it could for the Kingdom of Heaven.

2. Other Christians demonstrate too much involvement and interest. There are those who take spiritual warfare to an extreme. They see demons everywhere in everything. For example, if it rains, then it is the devil's fault, we can shower him with a lot of glory for something he has never done.

Spiritual warfare is not about shouting, it is about our authority. What is the difference? A parent shouts at their child, "Stop it!" But does the child take heed? It depends whether the parent exercised authority or just noise; as authority always delivers an end result. We must proclaim light and Truth to every part of our daily life.

The sadness is that some can lose their edge for Jesus because their focus is on the devil, demons, and the strategies of hell.

Evan Roberts lead a great revival for Wales in 1904. It has been reported over 100,000 people came to Christ in only a few months. Society was changed, as miners became tender loving husbands and fathers. However, as the revival progressed, Roberts started a personal study of hell and the devil. He wanted to uncover the organization of the demonic hierarchy because he felt the need to engage in spiritual warfare. His focus became darkness and not the light of Jesus. He quickly suffered from confusion and depression, and withdrew from the public eye. His ministry suffered as others tried to capitalize on his success. Soon most of the fruit of his revival had died and he lived the rest of his life in isolation, prior to his death in 1951. There is a lesson to be learned from Evan Roberts. My point - be aware of our spiritual enemy, but stay focused on Jesus.

3. This third area of error is when flesh and blood, rather than principalities and powers become the target. This is the most common of the mistakes made in spiritual warfare. It is easy to see a person as the enemy. It is a person who is talking bad about us. It is a person who refuses to cooperate with us. It is a person who is giving false teaching. It is a person who sells the drugs on the street corner. It is the person who is teaching evolution. It is the person who is preaching false doctrine. It is the person who is our boss at work, who tells us we cannot wear a cross, or put a little sign with a Bible verse on our desk. It is just too easy to focus on the person who is causing us anger and disappointment, rather than looking at the spirit guiding this person.

I believe today's best role models in spiritual warfare are the Christians in Moslem countries. The situation is so horrible that married couples have been arrested together and then the next day, the wife is released. She is told that she is still under investigation, and when the investigation is completed; she will go back to jail. This creates mental torture.

I have spoken to Christian pastors in Moslem lands who have told me that their elders keep getting arrested. In addition, some people have family members who have been killed by government hit-men. I have met with family members of those killed for their faith, and been astounded by their loving attitude. Their prayer is:

if they are ever murdered for being Christians, the love they show will draw their assailant into a personal relationship with Jesus Christ.

These future martyrs are like Steven in Acts 7:60 *'Then falling on his knees, he cried out with a loud voice, 'Lord, do not hold this sin against them!' Having said this, he fell asleep.'*

Paul and Silas were also such witnesses while in the Philippian jail as recorded in Acts.

'When they had struck them with many blows, they threw them into prison, commanding the jailer to guard them securely; and he, having received such a command, threw them into the inner prison and fastened their feet in the stocks. But about midnight Paul and Silas were praying and singing hymns of praise to God, and the prisoners were listening to them; and suddenly there came a great earthquake, so that the foundations of the prison house were shaken; and immediately all the doors were opened and everyone's chains were unfastened. When the jailer awoke and saw the prison doors opened, he drew his sword and was about to kill himself, supposing that the prisoners had escaped. But Paul cried out with a loud voice, saying, 'Do not harm yourself, for we are all here!' And he called for lights and rushed in, and trembling with fear he fell down before Paul and Silas, and after he brought them out, he said, 'Sirs, what must I do to be saved?' Acts 16:23-30

The joy of the Lord, in the midst of persecution, witnessed to the jailer, and drew him into wanting Jesus for himself and his family. Stephen, Paul, Silas and those saints in the Moslem nations all recognize our enemy is the unseen spirit, not the flesh and blood people who are standing in opposition. Their experiences show us spiritual warfare is for everyone. Just as the body of Christ has many members with different functions, the warfare waged against the principalities and powers will have much diversity. It is my prayer that as the many weapons are examined in the chapters which follow; all Christians will find their mission, which will glorify Jesus Christ as Lord.

CHAPTER 2

Strategic Warfare

Although this chapter will compare principles of military warfare with principles of spiritual warfare in order to provide a better understanding of strategic and tactical spiritual warfare. For those who have no understanding of military or war, I believe it is time to get our hands dirty and become the men and women that God wants us to be. For this to happen we must uncover "strategic warfare."

The term *"strategic"* needs clarification. Just as military forces and war planners deal with strategic and tactical situations, so does the Church of Jesus Christ, as we deal with demonic forces.

When I was in the United States Army, we trained diligently to gain expertise in tactics. Our armored personnel carriers would charge across a field, and then get into a wooded area, where my platoon would quickly disembark and charge up the hill. We would spend countless hours engaged in these exercises, with constant repetition.

Another basic tactic is known as "fire and maneuver." In this exercise an infantry squad consisting of two teams, is on patrol. Suddenly, someone in a machine gun nest begins shooting at them. Of course, the first thing to happen is they all hit (lay down on) the ground. Then as one team returns fire, the other team maneuvers into position, to attack the machine gun nest from the flank. Sometimes, the two groups change roles. If the group who is closing in on the flank hits a snag or gets pinned down, then they can start firing, and the other group begins to maneuver in the other direction. The plan is both groups close in, and eventually capture, or kill, those in opposition.

In spiritual warfare, there are many lessons that Christians can learn and practice from this simple exercise.

1.   When one team is confronting the enemy (by moving into position for direct confrontation), the other team is supporting by "firing on the enemy." When engaged in spiritual warfare, this support group can be praying against the powers of darkness. An example of such a tactic being used occurred one evening in our chapel coffee house at Cooke Barracks in Goeppingen, West Germany. A report came to the chapel that a member of our fellowship was being held in the Military Police (MP) station. The first action taken by a leader of the coffee house was for us to pray. It was then agreed that I should go to the MP station to see if I could help our brother. One group prayed in support while another made a face to face effort to make a difference.

Many Christian musical artists have a group in constant prayer while a new CD is being recorded in the studio. The Prison ministry, KAIROS, also asks for a prayer vigil to be conducted on the "outside" during the weekend of the ministry inside. Teaching, fellowship, and evangelism, are happening in the prison. Meanwhile there is always someone praying for them during the program, in support.

2.   Second, the soldiers in battle on the ground have a leader to give direction and encouragement. In the same way, pastors and ministry leaders provide direction and encouragement to those charged with their spiritual care. Our spiritual leaders need prayer for protection, and wisdom and strength to fulfill their task. In addition, Christians need to follow the directions of their spiritual leaders instead of resisting and/or opposing them. Most churches have horror stories of division because

of disloyalty toward their pastor. Pastors, on the other hand, need to stay focused on the mission and how to defeat the real enemy. Pastors need to put the needs of their people before their personal desires, like Jesus put our need of salvation in front of Himself. Good pastors love those in their congregations and lead them with love into a fruitful and victorious relationship with Jesus Christ.

In an actual combat situation, while soldiers are going face to face and toe to toe with the enemy infantry in front line warfare, there would be a host of combat related activities which would give them a strategic advantage. These strategic advantages would not be seen immediately, but over time could actually guarantee victory in the war.

As two small units engage in a skirmish, there could have been strategic activity leading into this day.

- The soldiers were recruited and trained. They are also provided proper equipment.

- The soldiers might have been given intelligence information about the location, morale, and strength of the enemy.

- The enemy might have been denied necessary equipment or replacement troops because of partisan guerrilla attacks on enemy supply lines.

- The enemy troops might have been shipped to another area by counter intelligence efforts to trick them into believing an attack was planned elsewhere.

When I was in the Army, there were countless hours of drill as we practiced fire and maneuver. Hundreds of times we would be on a patrol in training when suddenly, there was sniper fire. We would then go through the drill. One group would fire, the other maneuver. We practiced in daylight and darkness. We practiced in woods and open fields. We practiced in rain and sun. We did it so often, that should we have been called into combat we would know instinctively how to respond.

When the Church is trained to conduct spiritual warfare, we will recognize attacks from the enemy, and the proper way to respond quickly and effectively as a unit, driving the enemy back to where he belongs.

The sadness is that most activities in our congregations today are designed to entertain and inform, rather than to train and equip, so you walk as an overcomer.

For example, if the machine gun nest was larger and better fortified than the soldiers thought, they could use their radio to call headquarters and request artillery or aircraft support. A plane flying over and bombing the enemy machine gun nest would be involved, which can reflect intercession. Praying as your brothers and sisters go to war!

The strategic element played a major role in the tactical battle. The radios had to be built and transported to the battlefield, with provision made for communication between the ground and the air. The planes had to be built, pilots recruited and trained. Bombs had to be made and placed into the plane. Factories had to be built or redesigned to make the bombs, and the planes. Is there really any end as to how far back we can go to completely understand the concept of strategic warfare?

There is also more to strategic warfare behind the fire and maneuver described above. What if the ammunition factory of the enemy was bombed a few months before? And as a result, those in the machine gun nest were short of ammunition? What if the tank producing factory was bombed a year before? And as a result, the tanks which were supposed to be in formation in this area were not available. What if the counter-intelligence agents tricked the enemy into believing our forces were in another location? And as a result, most of the enemy moved elsewhere? The victory on that day, by the infantry squad, was possible only because of the strategic warfare conducted by hundreds if not thousands behind the scenes. While the bravery of the infantryman is not questioned, the role of the others behind the scenes has an equal part in the battle.

In a likewise manner, the church has need to operate more strategically than just the pastor, elders, and deacons. Many congregational members should be playing a strategic role in preparing and backing up the ministries of the congregation. For example, if there is to be a door to door campaign to invite potential new members, those gifted with writing, publishing, and photography, can play a much-needed supporting role to the outreach by using their gifts in the planning and preparation stages. The success or failure of the outreach could very well depend on those behind the scenes efforts.

Tactical Spiritual Warfare

Some examples of tactical spiritual warfare include, leading someone to Christ, casting out demons, prayer for healing and having true revival, such as the First and Second Great Awakenings in the USA, the Irish Revival of 1859, the Welsh Revival of the early 20th century, and the Jesus movement of the 1970s.

In each of these revivals, souls were saved and society was shaken, as huge multitudes came to know Jesus as Lord, and this influenced their community to live by biblical values. Every Christian should not just want to see revival, but be revival - salvation and deliverance every day to those around us. But the fact is that this does not happen. Why? It could very well be the reason that we are not successful in our tactical spiritual warfare, it is because we are neglecting the strategic part of spiritual warfare.

Winkie Pratney, evangelist from New Zealand, has done extensive study in church history. After examining revivals all over the world which span several centuries, he said, at the *Jesus '77* conference in Orlando, Florida, that the two requirements for revival are prayer and unity.

Many revivals in the 18th and 19th centuries can be traced back to the 110 year, 24 hours a day, 7 days a week prayer vigil in

Herrnhut, Germany by the Moravians. We will have a good look at this prayer vigil in the chapter on Herrnhut, but for now, we can appreciate the unity and prayer in Herrnhut as vital elements for revival. We need prayer and unity today more than ever. Therefore, we need to pray for others who are praying and we need to pray for the unity of all of those who are followers of Jesus. We desperately need to pray that the Lord draws us together and allow us to put aside the doctrines and practices which divide, in order for all Christians to focus on Jesus as Lord.

Front Line Warfare

As a World War Two buff, I have seen many maps showing the "front line" of the battle as the war progressed. In the beginning of the movie, *The Last 10 days of Hitler*, there is powerful music playing, and a map of Europe is shown. A big red area which represents Germany moves into Poland, then westward across the Netherlands, Belgium, Luxembourg and France. A few seconds later the red mass consumes Denmark and Norway. At one point the red is so large that it extends from France, North Africa, Italy, Greece, Eastern Europe and into the Soviet Union. Then it begins to shrink representing the Allied victories, until only a small spot of red at Berlin remains. The movie then begins with Adolph Hitler in his bunker in April 1945.

Most of our thoughts about war focus on what is happening at the places where the red ends. After all, it is where the actual shooting is taking place. It is where the artillery is hitting the soldiers in the foxholes. It is where the tank battles are raging. It is where the action is, but is it the only place where the action is?

The tactical war is going on at the front line. But there is plenty of activity behind the lines. There is warfare occurring in many more places than at the "front." There are the supply lines, the spy networks, the propaganda war to win the hearts and minds of the people involved, and many other actions taken by each side to strengthen the total war effort, and ultimately provide everything needed to those at the front line to win.

If we only look at the local tactical battles, we will fail to see the total picture. We may only react to the attacks of the enemy instead of going on the offensive and hitting him where he is weak. As Scripture states, '*The gates of Hades will not overpower it.*' (Church) (Matthew 16:18) We are to be on the offensive, and the purpose of this book is to put forth the idea that our strategic efforts are often a neglected offense.

In Ephesians 6, the apostle Paul writes that we are involved in spiritual warfare. He explains that we wrestle not against flesh and blood, but against principalities and powers. I consider myself to be somewhat of a military man. I completed Army ROTC (Reserve Officer Training Corps) in University, and was an officer in the United States Army. I have had the privilege of visiting many World War Two battlefields and sites. I have watched hundreds of documentaries on World War Two, and have prayerfully looked at the principles learned in our warfare against the powers of darkness.

When most people think of war, they think of the infantry soldier running towards the enemy surrounded by gunshots and bombs.

However, there is another part of warfare which is just as real, and in some ways more influential in the outcome of the war. This is strategic warfare of bombing the tank factories, and in a year from now, when he attacks the enemy and there are fewer tanks shooting back, it will make a difference.

In the midst of World War II, British intelligence agents in Bletchley Park, Milton Keynes, England, spent day and night sweating, studying, and examining codes from the German radios, for one purpose. If they could break the code, which they did do, it would help change the course of the war. They were on the front line as much as those who were in the trenches. You and I are on the front line as much as the pastor who is in the pulpit!

What is Strategic Warfare?

The dictionary defines "strategic" in a military sense, as an action intended to render the enemy incapable of making war. Wow, did you read that? Let's read it again… "Strategic" in a military sense, as an action intended to render the enemy incapable of making war. Now what did Jesus do? He took *'The keys of death and of Hades,'* (Revelation 1:18) rendering the devil powerless!

If we study the meaning further, it also means that by the destruction of materials, factories, etc., such as a strategic bombing mission, or any action which blocks the enemy's ability to provide essentials for the continuing conduct of a war.

In the course of this book, I will include examples of strategic missions, and how their success or failure affected the outcome of an important battle, or the war itself. This is to show how strategic warfare is vast, how vital strategic warfare is to the overall effort, and also how each person is involved in strategic spiritual warfare in some form.

However, the main focus in this book is to show the importance of strategic spiritual warfare. There are weapons of strategic spiritual warfare that the Lord has given us to wage effective measures against the powers of darkness. But also, we want to learn how to use these weapons for the greatest advantage, so that the Kingdom of Heaven can achieve success in every area of our lives.

Strategic plans can be long term, and results are not seen very quickly. Many of the current economic problems faced by governments around the world today, are in need of long term solutions. But the leaders are under severe pressure to find a quick solution to ease the suffering of the people, in order to remain in power or get re-elected. Unfortunately, the real challenge is to plan for the proper long term answer, rather than coming up with a half way solution which will only last until after the next election.

A look at many of the strategic "battles" of military warfare will reveal that results were not seen until perhaps years later. During the darkest days of World War Two, much planning and action was taking place behind the front lines. There was gathering of intelligence, production in armament factories, even the building of the atomic bomb.

In the same way, our strategic spiritual warfare efforts will not appear to be making any difference. "Mom" Ellis prayed for me for years, while in the natural world nothing was changing, in the Spirit world something was breaking!

The Lord has us on a journey not a sprint! There is the saying, "I asked the Lord for patience and I need it now!"

Strategic spiritual warfare can be for long periods of time, with little results, but know in Jesus, there is always a result!

The kingdom of darkness is like the fictional story that is told of Adolf Hitler, Benito Mussolini and Winston Churchill beside a large famous carp pond near Paris in the darkest, early days of World War Two. The three men reached an agreement that whoever could first catch one of the fish without a line or a net, would be the winner of the war. The other side would surrender and there would be no bloodshed.

As soon as the agreement was made, Adolph Hitler instructed Benito Mussolini to jump into the pond and grab one of those fish. Mussolini prided himself on being a top athlete with great physical skills. He dove into the water. He kept swimming around and down, grabbing at the fish who continued to elude his grasp. After only a few minutes, he was exhausted and feared he would not have the strength to even get out of the pond. As Mussolini dragged himself up the ladder and onto the patio, Adolph Hitler pulled out a pistol and began to shoot at the fish, but of course those rounds would deflect from the surface of the water and slowly sink to the bottom.

Winston Churchill kept observing this erratic behavior as he was sitting at a small table next to the pond, enjoying his afternoon tea. Adolph Hitler and Benito Mussolini, both exasperated and disgusted, looked at Churchill. They said, "It is not possible."

Churchill simply reached down into the pond with his teaspoon. He took a teaspoon full of water and flipped it into the nearby grass. Then he reached down and took another, then another. Hitler cried out, "What are you doing man?" Churchill smiles oh so smugly, "It may take a while, but we are going to win this war."

Obviously, one or two teaspoons of water from a large pond would not be noticed, but a constant effort would take all the water out eventually. As Christians pray, proclaim the Word, carry the Cross, use spiritual gifts, work in unity, participate in the sacraments, and live in righteousness; the Holy Spirit responds and wages the warfare to bring glory to Jesus Christ and victory to the Kingdom of Heaven.

In simple terms, strategic warfare is those actions which weaken the enemy in the long run. Dispersed throughout this book will be little explanations of actions taken in warfare which made a difference in the outcome of a war.

Sometimes, we can be focused on what the enemy is doing instead of seeing what God is doing. For in truth, we cannot defeat the devil by our strength, but through Christ.

For the purposes of our study, we want to learn how to provide spiritual support for the Church, especially the parts of the Church who are on the front lines of spiritual warfare. The Church, as a body, needs to weaken the powers of darkness. Working together, with each part functioning properly, Christianity can glorify Jesus, and proclaim His nature and character to the whole world.

'Return to the stronghold, O prisoners who have the hope; this very day I am declaring that I will restore double to you. For I will bend Judah as My bow. I will fill the bow with Ephraim. And I will stir up your sons, O Zion, against your sons, O Greece; and I will make you like a warrior's sword.' Zechariah 9:12-13

We are to attack worldly logic, and yet this logic has infiltrated the Church. Zechariah writes about the sons of Zion who are the people of God, being stirred as a warrior's sword to do battle against the sons of Greece. Greece was known in those days for logic. The world's logic often opposes the purposes of Jesus. There are those who are prisoners to world systems, world thought and world logic. The Church is to proclaim the Truth, the Gospel, and attack the sons of Greece. As we do, prisoners are set free. Knowledge and logic are good, but another level is God's logic, His understanding, His direction.

'For indeed Jews ask for signs and Greeks search for wisdom; but we preach Christ crucified, to Jews a stumbling block and to Gentiles foolishness.' 1 Corinthians 1:22-23

As the Church goes on the attack, we are fulfilling the words of Jesus when He said, *'I will build My church and the gates of Hades will not overcome it.'* Matthew 16:18

In the Bible days, "gates" was a place where gatekeepers allowed you entrance, or not, to the city. Elders would sit and rule from a place of authority, and yet Scripture states that the gates of hell will not prevail against the Church. Every Christian can successfully do battle against those who sit at the gates.

Our weapons include the Name of Jesus, the blood of Jesus, the cross, the Word, prayer, worship, humility, unity, spiritual gifts, forgiveness, proper use of sacraments, fasting, music and obedience. There is something for everyone as we embark on a fascinating journey in the world of strategic spiritual warfare.

One need not be a pastor, a missionary, a street preacher, Sunday school teacher, nor have a radio or television program to talk about Jesus, in order to be effective in spiritual warfare. There is an important role for every believer, and you can be encouraged to know that the Lord is eager to help you fulfill your role.

'I planted, Apollos watered, but God was causing the growth.' 1 Corinthians 3:6

Paul wrote this in the context of a division which existed between Christians who had split into camps favoring different Christian leaders. Some were following Paul, others Apollos, and still others were following other leaders, such as Peter.

Paul is saying, "Hold on folks. We are all working together. I started a process in the life of some; Apollos came along and shared about what Jesus did for him, but remember it was the Holy Spirit who was doing the real work."

There are many Christians in the public eye. There are many others on the front lines of spiritual warfare, battling in the halls of government, the underground church in Muslim controlled areas, and other places where the lost need to find Jesus Christ as their Lord. There are also many more not seen by the public, but who are indispensable to the building of the Kingdom of God. Wherever you are, your role is vital.

One final thought before ending this chapter concerns our daily priority of strategic work or tactical work. It is too easy for a pastor to get bogged down with everyday tasks such as preparing sermons, visiting members who are in hospital, and planning various programs. While these are important, a tragic result is that he then does not have the time, nor energy, to think and plan strategically. Retreats can be good to provide a way to take a few steps back, to look at the big picture, and plan new exciting approaches to win victory. However, too often, the pastor is the one planning the retreat, and he does not plan strategically. If you are a pastor or leader, how much of your day is spent tactically and how much is spent strategically?

CHAPTER 3

The devil's devices

'So that no advantage would be taken of us by Satan, for we are not ignorant of his schemes.' 2 Corinthians 2:11

Perhaps the Christians in Corinth in Paul's day had an understanding that most Christians of our time do not. I am not certain we are not ignorant of satan's schemes, because I think that the church today is often ignorant of what the devil is doing. In fact, in many Christian circles, it is not proper to even acknowledge the existence of the evil one or hell. It is appalling how many pastors will preach against the reality of hell.

Field Marshall Irvin Rommel had a great plan in his final battle in North Africa. He also had two problems. First, British Field Marshall, Bernard Law Montgomery, knew the plan because the allies broke the code via Enigma at Bletchley Park. Second, the Allies also knew when and where Rommel was getting his supplies via a navy convoy. Almost half of those ships were sunk by British submarines in the Mediterranean Sea. Rommel attacked and Montgomery was waiting. It became a trap. Nazi's were defeated badly and Rommel was called home. The victory was because the British were not ignorant of the Nazi schemes.

It is in the same in the spirit that the devil has many schemes, and it is wise for us to know them. A word of warning here, do not get focused on the devil, demons and powers of darkness. Stay focused on Jesus, but be wise in knowing how to deal with our spiritual enemy.

Evil spelled backward is live. Or a better way of thinking is, live spelled backward is evil. We should focus on living not on evil. At the same time, we must be aware that the devil exists and has a plan to destroy every Christian person and ministry.

'*Be of sober spirit, be on the alert. Your adversary, the devil, prowls around like a roaring lion, seeking someone to devour. But resist him, firm in your faith.*' 1 Peter 5:8-9

The devil is like a lion roaring, but a lion that has no teeth. For Jesus pulled his teeth with the victory at Calvary! When he roars, we will too often jump, but he only has the power you give him, he will use fear, intimidation and other mind games to sway us to yield to him, thus giving him power. One of the devil's big weapons is fear. The fear of death creates slavery to the devil.

'*…(Jesus) might free those who through fear of death were subject to slavery all their lives.*' Hebrews 2:15

There are many fears people suffer, fears that can create a barrier to service in the Kingdom of God. As a missionary, I can see how some fears can create a handicap and must be overcome in order to have an overcoming effectiveness level. One such fear can be flying. A missionary must travel long distances and often the only practical way to get to some places is by air. Claustrophobia is a common fear. Missionaries are often packed into planes, buses, trains, youth hostels, etc. Many rooms in foreign nations are very small and the missionary may be sharing the small room with several others. There are also fear of heights and fear of spiders or other small animals. Missionaries often stay in previously abandoned buildings that are quickly cleaned out to make room for the mission team.

Other fears are simply used by the devil to create havoc in the life of a Christian, and fear is manifested in so many different ways.

In preparing this section, I looked up "fear" in a thesaurus and found the following terms;

Fear: alarm, apprehension, abhorrence, agitation, anxiety, aversion, cold feet, cowardice, despair, dismay, distress, doubt, dread, horror, jitters, nightmares, panic, phobia, suspicion, timidity, worry, terrorize, intimidate, and hesitation.

Is the devil working in your life to create these traits? Worry comes from the devil, while the Lord gives confidence, hope and reassurance. In the Sermon on the Mount in Matthew 6, Jesus goes into detail about food, clothing and shelter. We are reminded that the Lord takes care of plants and animals, therefore; He will take care of you and I.

Words which relate to worry include apprehension, anxiety, dread, jitters, panic and trepidation. One of satan's devices is to create worry in our hearts and yet we need to conclude that worry changes nothing but us. Joshua may have had some concerns after Moses died, when God asked him to lead the people into the Promised Land. How do I know that? In Joshua one, the Lord tells Joshua four times to be strong and courageous. Joshua was feeling weak and worried. God was letting Joshua know that when we worry we do not trust!

'Be careful to do according to all the law.' Joshua 1:7

How many of these "fears" describe relationship issues? They include agitation, consternation, doubt, suspicion, to feel terrorized and intimidated. When we have fear in our heart, it will affect how we live in our families, workplaces and ministry. Trust issues will surface if there are doubts growing from seeds planted by the devil.

Nightmares

Some attacks by the devil may even seem unfair, such as nightmares. How can we defend ourselves while we are sleeping?

When we understand, the devil does not have evil, he is evil, then nothing "good" can come from him. The good news is; we can have victory, even over nightmares. A few practical preventatives include an awareness of what we are putting into our minds prior to sleep. Certain television shows, movies, music, or conversations may invite dark forces into our mind, and should be avoided as much as possible. A simple rule of thumb is that if Jesus walked into the TV room, would you be honored or ashamed?

We can also ask the Lord to watch over us while we sleep. We can ask other Christians to pray with us, and for us, creating a partnership against the enemy. Those prayers may include praying for spiritual cleansing in the room where sleep is occurring. If there are forces of darkness lingering, prayer for the light and love of Jesus will drive them out. Are there demonic books, magazines, movies, music, art work, figurines or other materials present in the room? If so, then simply remove them and if possible burn them. I seem to recall a story I heard about someone whose teenager was having nightmares because there was a heavy metal rock album with a demonic worshiping ritual on the cover. When the music and the album cover were removed, the nightmares ceased.

Every Christian must be very careful in this regard. The Bible tells us we are not to be ignorant of the devil's devices. We are to know what the enemy is doing. Then we can come in the opposite spirit and gain the victory.

Atheism

The definition of atheism has changed over the years. In former days, an atheist was simply someone who did not believe that there was a God. But today, the times have changed and changed drastically. Today, an atheist not only believes that there is no God, but anyone who does believe in God is dangerous, and must be stopped. Are we created in the image of God or are we simply creatures of time, chance and matter? The answer to this is crucial.

The passage Paul writes in 2 Corinthians has a connection to forgiveness.

'*But one whom you forgive anything, I* forgive *also; for indeed what I have forgiven, if I have forgiven anything,* I did it *for your sakes in the presence of Christ.*' 2 Corinthians 2:10

When we forgive, we are defeating satan and his plans to allow division to be in our hearts. He also wants to keep us in bondage to bitterness, and to be incapable of forgiveness, to focus on our hurt, instead of on our Healer.

As human beings we face three enemies: The world, the flesh, and the devil.

'*For all that is in the world, the lust of the flesh and the lust of the eyes and the boastful pride of life, is not from the Father, but is from the world.*' 1 John 2:16

The world is actually the devil's domain, and we will discuss this more fully in the next chapter.

Jesus answered, '*My kingdom is not of this world. If my kingdom were of this world, then My servants would be fighting so that I would not be handed over to the Jews; but as it is, My kingdom is not of this realm.*' John 18:36

'*And do not be conformed to this world, but be transformed by the renewing of your mind, so that you may prove what the will of God is, that which is good and acceptable and perfect.*' Romans 12:2

A fearful verse in the Bible to me is John 3:19. In John 3:16, Jesus proclaims "*God so loved the world.*" In John 3:19, Jesus explains men love darkness rather than the light. In the Greek several words translate as "love". Agape is usually defined as God's love. But to call agape God's love is not really an accurate description of agape. Agape is a total, giving, self-sacrificing love which was best demonstrated by Jesus' death on the cross. But here is the scary part, John 3:19 says people loved "agape", the darkness rather than the light!

Sinful man, who is us, will give everything, including life itself for darkness. Those who work with addictive personalities can easily understand this truth. The addiction so controls the addict that he will continue to practice the addiction regardless of the consequences. There is such a focus on alcohol, drugs, gambling or sex, (to name a few addictions specifically) the threat of bankruptcy, imprisonment, loss of family, or even death, is ignored.

In fact, I think that there is a pattern to the devil's plans to destroy a ministry before it can even get started. Remember the birth of Moses and Jesus?

'All things are lawful for me, but not all things are profitable. All things are lawful for me, but I will not be mastered by anything.' 1Corinthians 6:12

Then, for the remainder of this chapter, Paul mentions two problem areas we know can turn into addictions. The first is food, the second is sex. But this only scratches the surface when looking at the vast number of addictions which can cripple a Christian. There are so called "self-help" groups allowing those with specific addictions to gain strength. In these groups, there are mentors or sponsors, who are individuals available in moments of crisis.

There are even examples of this in the Bible, such as Noah, starting in Genesis 5. It appears that Noah may have been the only person who walked with the Lord in his day. A study of Noah's life can be a wonderful study of fellowship with Jesus. They did not just sit around praying and studying the Bible. Noah and Jesus worked together on several projects. First, they built a huge boat, even though Noah's neighbors did not understand.

Then after they finished the boat, I could hear Noah say it was fun and he wanted to build another, but Jesus had an idea for a new project. How about zoology? Adam liked to name the animals with the Lord, maybe Noah would like to collect them. So, the Lord brought every kind of animal to Noah, and they all got on the boat.

Then for about a whole year, Noah, his family, all those animals and the Lord, went sailing together. It was great fun. It is always fun to do things with Jesus. Christianity is not dry, dull, boring stuff, it is exciting.

After the sailing time was over, Noah and the Lord decided to get into farming together. Noah grew a vineyard, but then unfortunately Noah found the buzz he got from the wine was more fun than being with the Lord. The sad truth is that we never hear about Noah and the Lord having fellowship afterward. The world will always make attempts to strangle the spiritual life out of a Christian by making something in the world more pleasing than a relationship with Jesus

Here is only a partial list of addictions: alcohol, drugs, sex, gambling, shopping, food (overeaters anonymous) and computer games.

I do not know of any "I play too many computer games anonymous" groups, but, I list it because I know I have wasted days, if not months, or perhaps a year of my life, playing games on the computer. Many times, I need to prepare a sermon, or write something important on the word processor. But I think to myself, "First a quick game of chess."

Suddenly, I notice an hour has gone by and no work has been done. The same can be said about newspaper crossword puzzles and Sudoku. How much time gets wasted while the clock of life is ticking?

To properly engage in spiritual warfare and have the victorious Christian life, we must have victory over our habits and time. Each Christian has various and different temptations. All of us should seek the Lord, to show us where the challenges lie and how He can help us overcome.

What are some weapons that the devil has developed to attack the authority of Christ? I want to take a brief look at five of them.

Evolution

I had the joy of participating in a mission trip to Armenia. We worked construction during the week and had some wonderful trips on the weekend to see the sights there. While on our way to Mt. Ararat, a young man who is being home schooled by Christian parents, began speaking to a couple of people on our mission trip. One was a retired primary school principal and the other a lab manager in a hospital. He was talking about creation and how it was true, and evolution was false. These two Christian leaders were quite rude and dogmatic about how wrong he was. I entered the conversation giving a few facts of science, which gave credence to the theory of creation. Immediately, the lab manager back peddled and proclaimed that it really does not matter. Of course, her tone towards this young man seemed to matter as she tried to dissuade him from his beliefs. I told her that it does matter because thousands of people will decide against the Truth of the Bible because of the theory of evolution. In the very interesting movie/documentary, *Expelled*, Ben Stein interviews Richard Dawkins. Dawkins freely admits that he is an atheist because of his belief in the theory of evolution. So, obviously it matters to Dawkins.

Why should it matter? Our battle against the devil includes the efforts made by the powers of darkness to promote a world view which excludes Christian truth. If Genesis is not true, then how can we trust the accounts of miracles to be true? If the miracles we know about from Scripture never took place, then how can we trust the resurrection of Jesus Christ? And if Jesus Christ was not raised from the dead, then we are still in our sins.

Another truth which the lie of evolution seeks to destroy is that we are created in the image of God. Because all people are created in His image, then every person has value. In generations past, children were taught in government schools that they were created in the image of God. In fact, the Holy Bible was used as a text book and basic Bible principles were taught as recently as the 1940's in

Texas. These Christian values were a part of a larger teaching of the value of each human being. Respect and self-confidence was taught as a by-product of this foundation.

Today, most if not all government school systems are afraid of lawsuits, plus, they do not know the Constitution of the United States, which mandates the government cannot restrict the freedom of Religion. All too many people think that the Constitution says that there must be a separation of Church and State.

Therefore, nothing Christian can have any influence in the public arena. This tool of the devil, plotted a long time ago and slowly brought into majority approval, has resulted in the students being taught the exact opposite of the Bible world view. A trip to the children's section of any bookstore will discover books on "prehistoric dinosaurs." In fact, it is a popular topic for children. It seems movies such as *Jurassic Park* have increased the interest in dinosaurs in the minds of many children. Dinosaurs are a big sale item from toys, to posters and to books.

On the first page of many of these books will be the phrase, "billions of years ago...." The lies are being drilled into the minds, hearts and spirits of children. To repeat again what Adolph Hitler is credited as saying, "If you tell a lie often enough, people will believe it to be the truth."

Instead of being created in the image of God, resulting in respect for all people and an understanding of their own intrinsic value; today's government school children are taught that they are the result of random atoms bumping around, that they are the result of chemicals swirled in a volcanic soup billions of years ago. They are taught that they are merely a load of enzymes which should eventually return to the earth, decay and feed the next generation. They are taught that they do not have a spirit or an eternal soul. Therefore there is no reason to respect anyone else or themselves.

I have spent much of my life ministering in jails, prisons and mental hospitals. I have observed first-hand the result of Darwin's theory, which is believed and followed by so many young people. They are convinced that there is no spiritual realm. The best they can hope for is to live their lives doing what they want because they do not have an eternal soul. Many are driven to suicide because of the hopelessness and despair resulting from the embrace of evolution by our society.

Do we need to ask, Is the Bible true? Is the Bible a source we can trust? If the Bible is untrue about creation, then can it be true about Jesus and the resurrection? If the Bible is untrue about creation, then are we free to ignore the moral teachings of the Ten Commandments? If the Bible is untrue about creation, then are we really forgiven from our sins? If the Bible is untrue about creation, then do we have assurance of our salvation?

The Bible is one of our chief weapons of strategic spiritual warfare. The devil would like nothing better than for Christians to doubt its power and truth, thus negating the effectiveness of the Word as a weapon against him.

Diversity

There is a need for unity in the Body of Christ, with diversity. The world consists of many different types of people. There are differences in age, race, culture, music preference, financial status, religion, doctrine within each religion, hair color, shoe sizes and the list goes on and on. There are over five billion people living now and each one is different, which screams we live in a diverse world.

But there is a difference in the world view of diversity and the Biblical view of diversity. The Bible tells us we are the body of Christ; one body with many parts. The apostle Paul in I Corinthians 12 explains that there are no unimportant parts of the human body. Each part has a special function and when all the body parts are functioning as they should it is called healthy. When a portion of the body fails to function, it is called sickness. But each part is in the body and spiritually speaking each of us must be in the Body of Christ to be healthy. Jesus is our highest common denominator as we seek unity during diversity.

The world wants to promote diversity without Jesus. In fact, in many plans calling for the celebration of diversity, there does not appear to be any point of unity because the devil is promoting the celebration of division in the world, for unity is not part of him.

Open Minded

Being open minded is another politically correct buzz term used these days. Certainly Christians should not be prideful, bigoted or harsh. Christians should be humble, loving, and learners. There is a limit as to how open our minds should be. I heard a slogan once: "If you are too open minded, no telling what might fall into your mind. The spiritual gift of discernment is necessary in order to properly accept what is light and reject what is of darkness. We cannot be "open" to everything.

No Absolutes

Flexibility seems to be a theme in the devil's bag of tricks. We are told of the importance of diversity and being open minded. We are living in a new modern world. Slogans such as "If it feels good do it" and "Different strokes for different folks" are heard loud and often. We are taught not to use words such as "always" or "never." Different circumstances and different problems require different solutions. There are no absolutes in today's world.

Something I heard Winkie Pratney say at *Jesus '77* was that in the future (and the future is now) you can be anything you want to be. You can say anything you want to say, you can believe anything you want to believe. Only one requirement, you cannot try to make anyone else believe what you do. We must be accepting and tolerant of everyone's beliefs. Nobody is wrong.

Of course if you are a Christian, and a Bible Christian, then we must do what Jesus told us to do. Jesus told us to go and teach others what He taught us.

The Media

The media has great power. Those in control of newspapers, magazines, television and the movies can exert great influence over the hearts and minds of the masses, Hitler has been credited by some as saying that if you tell a lie often enough then it will be taken as truth. One only needs to examine the life of Joseph Goebbels and his role as Propaganda Minister in Nazi Germany to see how the power of the media can be used for evil.

When *Gone with the Wind* concluded with Rhett Butler telling Scarlett O'Hara that he did not "give a damn," it caused ripples everywhere. Such language apparently had never been used before. Now most movies have all kinds of horrible language. It is so expected if a war movie, prison movie, or movies about street people, do not contain a lot of vulgarity, they are criticized when reviewed.

We must also see in many movies today that there is a deliberate attempt to make the Christian the "bad guy." When I was a pastor years ago, we were approached by a film crew who wanted to use our church building for some scenes in their movie. We were assured it was a good film about a Christian woman who wanted to obey the teachings of the Bible. It was a delightful film with many good scenes where the audience is challenged to reach out to others in the name of Jesus. However, the pastor of the church was seen as a hypocrite and unloving. He opposed the work of his member in trying to help a young man who had been arrested. While the woman was a hero, the pastor and other church members were portrayed as unloving, uncaring and/or out of touch with the realities of the day.

My point in this is to say that the devil had plans many years ago to use the media and film industry to turn hearts away from Jesus and we must admit that he has been successful. I will be using scenes of many movies to provide examples for points being made in the study of strategic spiritual warfare, which only proves how powerful the media can be. Just remind yourself that not that long ago there were certain things not acceptable to the TV censors watchdog. But now it is more acceptable to our society because of media influence. It gives credence to not be married, homosexuality, adultery and affairs. Christians approve of it by watching the program or buying the DVD to watch them.

I am totally appalled how certain scenes in 18 certified movies have been reduced to 15-year-old viewing. Many of the 15 certified movies have now been reduced to 12-year-old viewing, and have you ever asked why?

The devil is using the media to take his evil and impurities, and to reach our children. When shared, once it becomes normal as such, it is then accepted. The sadness is that even churches now have accepted what the Bible calls wrong, because of a generational change in thinking.

Yes, the devil has a plan to destroy the world and the Kingdom of Heaven. Often it looks like he is succeeding and Christians are tempted to merely smile, open the Bible to Revelation, and smugly exclaim, in the back of the book we win. But it will never be won through weakness, but instead by being an overcomer in Christ.

Jesus has assured the final victory in this war. But there are many battles which can be lost between now and when Jesus returns. For us to see our future blood line be stronger than we are, we need to overcome the goliath we face so that our children are not fighting the devil that we were to defeat.

Christians must engage the powers of darkness in spiritual warfare. The purpose of this work is to encourage and equip the Church to wisely gain victory on every front.

This means gaining an understanding of how the devil wants to use a long term strategy to discredit Christianity, and then going on the attack to bind those powers of darkness, and bring light and love into our society.

The devil also has schemes to bring defeat to each individual and claim their soul for his dark purposes. These are to be prayer points. In prayer we can bring the Holy Spirit into a situation where the devil is trying to manipulate and destroy. A prayer focused on the life-giving power of Jesus will bring victory.

As Scripture states in John 10:10, '*The thief comes only to steal and kill and destroy; I came that they may have life, and have it abundantly.*'

The devil can attack individual people and families with divorce, fear, confusion and/or suicide. There are family curses which need to be identified and broken. One such curse is when you see sons in prison of which their fathers had also entered the penal system and in some cases also their grandfathers.

For a time, I served in the ministry of *Malachi Men* in a Kentucky prison, with my friend Stan Bramblett.

We taught Christian principles to men in prison, over a long series of programs. Then almost as a graduation, the prison authorized a Saturday afternoon where the inmate's children could spend the day with their dads.

The concept was simple, to create a spiritual atmosphere in the family which would break the demonic curse and bring wholeness to the children involved. *Malachi Men* is aggressively changing the patterns of families to bring hope and wholeness to future generations. The work of *Malachi Men* will bring strategic victories for the Kingdom of Heaven for future generations.

Just as the devil has been plotting and planning for the destruction of future generations, the Church must be prayerfully planning to win the spiritual battles of tomorrow, and give a better chance to our children.

CHAPTER 4

Battlefield & Domain

Warning! This chapter is for those who wish to overcome!

'For our struggle is not against flesh and blood, but against the rulers, against the powers, against the world forces of wickedness in the heavenly places.' Ephesians 6:12

The battlefield we fight on is not natural, but spiritual. It is not visible, but invisible (except the Lord opens our eyes - 2nd Kings 6:17).

So using a military parallel, we are living as soldiers surrounded by the enemy, and we need to watch our step carefully. But it is nothing to be fearful of, but we do have to be wise.

We face a constant portrayal of the damaging traits of the enemy presented in a positive way. For instance, the manipulation can be seen in beer commercials. They are created to show fun and contain people laughing and having a good time. The purpose of the commercial is to sow into the viewer that if fun is the goal then you need to drink this brand of beer. The sadness is that too much beer destroys families, relationships, and even lives.

The devil wants us to be worldly, not live like citizens of the Kingdom of Heaven. Consider the following Scriptures…

'Jesus answered, 'My kingdom is not of this world. If My kingdom were of this world, then My servants would be fighting so that I would not be handed over to the Jews; but as it is, My kingdom is not of this realm.' Therefore Pilate said to Him, 'So You are a king?' Jesus answered, 'You say correctly that I am a king. For this I have been born, and for this I have come into the world, to testify to the truth. Everyone who is of the truth hears My voice.' John 18:36-37

Jesus declares before Pilate, that His Kingdom is not an Earthly Kingdom, but Heavenly. Consequently, we can never get too comfortable with our Earthly surroundings.

'Thus I will punish the world for its evil and the wicked for their iniquity; I will also put an end to the arrogance of the proud and abase the haughtiness of the ruthless.' Isaiah 13:11

Pride is a world characteristic, while humility, another strategic weapon, is a Christian characteristic.

Jesus said, 'You are the light of the world. A city set on a hill cannot be hidden.' Matthew 5:14

As Christians, we are to shine the light of Jesus into the world.

'And the one on whom seed was sown among the thorns, this is the man who hears the word, and the worry of the world and the deceitfulness of wealth choke the word, and it becomes unfruitful.' Matthew 13:22

This is from the parable of the soils (as I call it). As we live like the world, with its worries and deceitful ways, we lose our ability to be fruitful for the Kingdom of Heaven.

Jesus said, 'For what will it profit a man if he gains the whole world and forfeits his soul? Or what will a man give in exchange for his soul?' Matthew 16:26

It is interesting and sad how many Christians will seek success and prosperity in the world at the risk of our relationship with Jesus Christ. This is often a subtle temptation which most of us have embraced at some point in our lives. Thank the Lord, for opening our eyes and giving us the strength to renounce the world.

Jesus said, *'The world cannot hate you, but it hates Me because I testify of it, that its deeds are evil.'* John 7:7

The world hates Jesus. We can therefore expect problems in the world.

Jesus said, *'If anyone hears My sayings and does not keep them, I do not judge him; for I did not come to judge the world, but to save the world.'* John 12:47

There is a plan to bring the world under the authority of Jesus Christ and the Kingdom of Heaven. Jesus wants the world to be saved. However, at present the world is under the domain of the devil, and our role is to shine the light of Truth in Jesus Christ, into the world in which we live.

Jesus said, *'Peace I leave with you; My peace I give to you; not as the world gives do I give to you. Do not let your heart be troubled, nor let it be fearful.'* John 14:27

The world does not bring peace. The world only brings confusion, heartache, fear and tribulation.

Jesus said, *'These things I have spoken to you, so that in Me you may have peace. In the world you have tribulation, but take courage; I have overcome the world.'* John 16:33

Jesus tells us clearly that we can walk confidently because He has promised us victory, while yet we can be surrounded by those who oppose Jesus and everything that He stands for. They will lie and manipulate to twist the truth and give the impression that the devil is right and Jesus is wrong.

Jesus prayed the night of His betrayal and arrest. His prayer is recorded in John 17 and has many references to the world. It is enlightening to read and meditate on His prayer.

'I have manifested your Name to the men whom you gave me out of the world. They were yours and you gave them to me, and they have kept your word. I ask on their behalf. I do not ask on behalf of the world, but of those whom you have given me, for they are yours. I am no longer in the world, and yet they themselves are in the world. And I come to You Holy Father, keep them in your Name, the Name which you have given me, that they may be one even as we are. But now I come to you; and these things I speak in the world so that they may have my joy made full in themselves. I have given them your Word; and the world has hated them, because they are not of the world, even as I am not of the world. I do not ask you to take them out of the world, but to keep them from the evil one. They are not of the world, even as I am not of the world. As You sent Me into the world, I also have sent them into the world that they may all be one, even as You, Father, are in Me and I in You, that they also may be in Us, so that the world may believe that You sent Me. I in them and You in Me, that they may be perfected in unity, so that the world may know that You sent me, and loved them, even as You have loved Me. Father, I desire that they also, whom You have given Me, be with Me where I am, so that they may see My glory which You have given Me, for You loved Me before the foundation of the world. O righteous Father, although the world has not known You, yet I have known You; and these have known that You sent Me.'

John 17:6, 9, 11, 13-16, 18, 21, 23-25.

The devil Manipulates the World

Scriptures show us the devil is at work in the world, and this is the reason Christians need to be bold in taking the world back for the Kingdom of Heaven, and away from the devil.

Jesus said, *'Now judgment is upon this world; now the ruler of this world will be cast out.'* John 12:31

'In whose case the god of this world has blinded the minds of the

unbelieving so that they might not see the light of the gospel of the glory of Christ, who is the image of God.' 2 Corinthians 4:4

'And you were dead in your trespasses and sins, in which you formerly walked according to the course of this world, according to the prince of the power of the air, of the spirit that is now working in the sons of disobedience.' Ephesians 2:1-2

'...and every spirit that does not confess Jesus is not from God; this is the spirit of the antichrist, of which you have heard that it is coming, and now it is already in the world.' 1 John 4:3

'We know that we are of God, and that the whole world lies in the power of the evil one.' 1 John 5:19

'If you were of the world, the world would love its own; but because you are not of the world, but I chose you out of the world, because of this the world hates you.' John 15:19

We should not be shocked when we see militant atheism, homosexuality running rampant, abortion advocates using extreme rhetoric against Christians and lying about what happens in an abortion clinic, and the pro-Moslem/anti-Christian polices of many governments and businesses, as the devil seeks to establish his kingdom.

The Bible gives us an unusual promise. *'In the world you will have tribulation.'* (John 16:33) I know Jesus went on to say "fear not" because He overcame the world. But it does not negate the fact that in the world we will have tribulation.

It amazes me how Christians are so unprepared for tribulation. It amazes me even more how Christians refuse to acknowledge tribulation is a big part of our Earthly lives. We expect to be blessed and sheltered against all troubles.

Let me explain two things about tribulation. First there are normal everyday problems that Christians will face as we seek to walk in total obedience to the teachings of Jesus. John is perhaps the best example as he mentions tribulation twice in the opening chapters of Revelation.

'I, John, your brother and fellow partaker in the tribulation and kingdom and perseverance which are in Jesus, was on the island called Patmos because of the word of God and the testimony of Jesus.' Revelation 1:9

'I know your tribulation and your poverty... Do not fear what you are about to suffer. Behold, the devil is about to cast some of you into prison, so that you will be tested, and you will have tribulation for ten days. Be faithful until death, and I will give you the crown of life.' Revelation 2:9-10

Second, there is what is known in some circles as, "The Great Tribulation."

'For then there will be a great tribulation, such as has not occurred since the beginning of the world until now, nor ever will.' Matthew 24:21

'... These are the ones who come out of the great tribulation, and they have washed their robes and made them white in the blood of the Lamb.' Revelation 7:14

I believe that much of our beliefs about the Coming of Jesus/ Rapture are based on our denial that tribulation is not part of the Christian life. Many Christians simply think that before things get too bad that Jesus will come and snatch them away to Heaven. This is foolish thinking.

There is a movement of people who promote what has been called the "Prosperity Gospel." The roots of this teaching are born out of "self" and not Christ. How do I know that? Because we are taught that our spirituality is proven by living in a bigger house, driving a more expensive car, having finer clothes, exotic vacations, and all to prove we are better than our neighbor. If you believe in that type of prosperity message, then do yourself a favor; read the Bible without the prosperity glasses on and you will see even in the Book of Acts when the church was born; Christians suffered, were persecuted and some laid their life down. Now is this the prospering you were told about?

A couple of years ago, I went to various Churches to promote world missions. I attended a Sunday morning service at a neighborhood church of a friend. The message was the "Prosperity Gospel" and one thing I noticed, they could not care less about missions. They could not understand why everyone simply does not have "faith" that Jesus would provide them with abundant overflowing wealth. I have reached the conclusion that if a message cannot be preached in a concentration camp, it should not be preached in the wealthy suburbs.

In fact, prosperity preachers "have", while their people "have not." This is not Kingdom life, nor will it be Heaven life. The time for "send me and the Lord will bless you" is over, awake to the scrupulous spiritual thieves who proclaimed, "if you give to God then God will pay yours." Of course, he meant, "If you send me money, then look for God to pay your obligations."

Our Role in the World

'Pure and undefiled religion in the sight of our God and Father is this: to visit orphans and widows in their distress, and keep oneself unstained by the world.' James 1:27

Systems cannot love, and world systems are actively at work destroying lives, especially the lives of the neediest. The Church has a history of helping those with the most need. Hospitals and schools were founded originally by the Church. In fact, much of the medical care crisis that the world faces today is because the government took over healthcare, and made it so difficult for the Church to maintain its role. The same can be said about the school system. The government-run schools have not only taken over the education of our children, but by the exclusion of Christian teaching and Christian values, have made a conscious effort to prevent students from embracing Jesus.

'Do not love the world nor the things in the world. If anyone loves the world, the love of the Father is not in him.' 1 John 2:15

'You are from God, little children, and have overcome them; because greater is He who is in you than he who is in the world.' 1 John 4:4

'You adulteresses, do you not know that friendship with the world is hostility toward God? Therefore whoever wishes to be a friend of the world makes himself an enemy of God.' James 4:4

'And do not be conformed to this world, but be transformed by the renewing of your mind, so that you may prove what the will of God is, that which is good and acceptable and perfect.' Romans 12:2

Just as Jesus prayed the night of His arrest, we are to be in the world, but not of the world, which is so easy to say and difficult to fulfill.

In Romans 12:2, *'do not be conformed to this world'* should be translated as "do not let the world squeeze you into its mold", in order to be true to the Greek text.

This passage describes a deliberate action on the part of the world to take a Christian and actively seek to change him. I can picture a Christian that is not aware of the enemy's intention, being picked up and pushed into a world shaped container and being forced to becoming the same shape as the world.

Even listing the ways of the world can be controversial because there are so many Christians who will accuse one of being narrow minded and/or legalistic.

Yet the standard of 'Christianity' has dropped so far that in many churches one finds it difficult to discern between the church service or an entertainment club with the smoke, flash spotlights, noise etc. In fact we have raised a generation of believers who believe that is church; when in fact Jesus never died for that. He died that we would walk in the power of God, not in the trappings of this world

These churches portray that it is normal for divorce, tattoos and piercings on bodies, sex before marriage, living together is much too common, the use of vulgar words and terms, or perhaps only change a letter of the vulgar word but the meaning is obviously the same. Simply put, they pat you on the back and say – "God understands!" I say "Yes, God understood it so much that He sent His Son so that we are transformed from the world, not into the world."

Scripture says, '...*the little foxes that are ruining the vineyards.*' (Song of Solomon 2:15) Little things can destroy the big things that God has planned for you. Thinking long term will help you make decisions short term. According to Josh McDowell in his tape series, *Belief Matters*, the teenage pregnancy rate is not much different between Christian teens active in their congregations and those not claiming to be Christian. For the Church to be salt and light to the world, we must be separate from the world systems and philosophies

Many Christians allow their political party to be their Lord, rather than Jesus. We need to ask ourselves, "When my political group takes a stand which conflicts with the Bible, do I oppose my political group?" "When engaging in Political debate, do I seek to show love and respect in the way Jesus would?"

For those who maybe believe that God would not want you as a Christian to be in ministry and still work, just remember Paul who had a real Jesus encounter, visions, wrote 13 books of the New Testament, worked as required... '*and because he was of the same craft, he lodged with them and worked; for by their occupation they were tentmakers.*' (Acts 18:3)

Christians should be involved in offices of Presidents, Senators, Congressmen, Governors, State Representatives, etc. We should be the ones who set the standard of quality workmanship, after all God lives within!

When at *Youth with a Mission*, Orlando, Florida, I heard Dean Sherman speak of our need to have spiritual radar which circles our minds. This spiritual radar seeks to locate and recognize any thought headed in our direction which is worldly. Those thoughts and ways must be rejected in order for us to have Kingdom thoughts and Kingdom ways.

As we are being made aware throughout this book, we are at war. But our warfare is not against flesh and bone, but principalities and powers. This war is serious business and must be waged wisely, and against the proper enemy. We must use Kingdom of Heaven weapons and not worldly weapons. One main purpose of this book is an examination of Kingdom of Heaven weapons.

As shared somewhat earlier; there is a debate among Christians about the last days. Some believe, as Christians increasingly become the light of the world, that the Kingdom of Heaven will be established on earth and everyone will follow Jesus. Others think that the world will become increasingly evil, that Jesus Christ will return to eradicate the evil and He sets up His Earthly Kingdom after defeating all His foes. I am also sure there are many other beliefs.

Regardless of which belief you adhere to. The truth is, we live in a world ruled by darkness. Yet our role is to live in the light, proclaim the light knowing God's light will defeat the darkness. A day will soon be on us when Light will rule and the domain of darkness will no longer exist. For now, we must seek to win the individual spiritual battles for the souls of men and the destiny of nations. As our individual battles are won, we gain confidence and experience to face the challenges of tomorrow.

David is a good example; he faced Goliath after overcoming a lion, and then a bear that had attacked the sheep in his care. Israel won the victory through David against Goliath and his army that day because of the leadership David provided. Like David, we wage this war fully aware that we are surrounded by enemies and yet under God – the giants are already defeated.

CHAPTER 5

The Church & The Jews

Anyone needing proof of the devil need only study the history of the Chosen people of the Lord, the Jews. It is an interesting journey which begins in the Garden of Eden. At the time of the fall, when sin entered the world and death would be the fate of all people, the Lord promised Adam and Eve one day that the seed of the woman would provide redemption. The devil immediately and consistently began an attack which continues with great violence to this day.

The vicious attack of the devil against the Jews has been ideological, violent, and devious. We can see it numerous times in Scripture and in world history. While in Egypt, Pharaoh issued an order for all Jewish boy babies to be killed, which would result in that the male deliverer being born would be annihilated. In Kings and Chronicles we read how the Assyrians conquered Israel (not Judea) and scattered the Jewish people in many directions. Then Nebuchadnezzar invaded Jerusalem a few generations later, to destroy the Temple and bring the Jews to Babylon. Remember Esther? She lived in the Persian Empire when a decree went out at the suggestion of the wicked Haman for the extermination of all the Jews in the kingdom (which would have been all the Jews in the world).

After the first coming of Jesus, the New Testament explained that it would be the Jews holding the key to the Second Coming of Jesus and the End of the Age. It would be after the re-establishment of Israel and in response to the savage attack made against Jerusalem by her enemies that Jesus comes back. Therefore, the devil had a plan to prevent the Jews from having a homeland. If the Jews could be destroyed, such as the Holocaust attempted, then Jesus' plan would be thwarted.

The early Church became proud and began an assault against the Jews, claiming Christians had replaced the Jews as the Chosen People. In fact, some taught that when the Bible stated a promise granted to Israel, it should be interpreted as the Church instead of Israel. It needs to be made clear: there is nothing anywhere in the Bible saying that the Church has replaced the Jews as the Chosen People. Every teaching which declares this is a false teaching and every preacher who declares it is a false prophet!

As the early church moved out of the persecution stage because of the Roman Emperor Constantine, many leaders began an attack against the Jews. These attacks included the false teaching that the Jews killed Jesus. There were also decrees to make the Jews suffer, such as converting to Judaism being punishable by death; Jews were disqualified from serving in the military or holding high government office. Sunday was made the Holy Day and no work was permitted. In many nations such as Egypt and Spain, the Church leaders took property away from the Jews and expelled them from the land. The devil used highly motivated Christians in his attempt to destroy the Jews.

Even to this day, there are many Christians blinded and deceived as they support the enemies of Israel. They deny Israel the right to defend herself against the massive forces of Islam. Israel is surrounded by enemy nations who have been attacking Israel non-stop since 1948.

When churches teach, or have a belief against Israel which could be classed as a "Replacement Theology," it is the foundation for much of this anti-Semitism. There is a real danger for those siding with the enemies of Israel. Numbers 24:9 clearly states that those who bless Israel will be blessed and those who curse Israel will be cursed. God was not referring to "Church" here. Again, a study of World History will show many nations who cursed Israel now no longer exist, and many who exist are shadows of their former glory. Those gone include the Roman Empire, Nazi Germany, the Soviet Union, Assyria, the Babylon Empire and the Persian Empire. Those who lost their role as a world super power include Egypt and the British Empire.

God Himself promises Israel the following…

'No weapon that is formed against you will prosper.' Isaiah 54:17

'O God, do not remain quiet; Do not be silent and, O God, do not be still. For behold, Your enemies make an uproar, And those who hate You have exalted themselves. They make shrewd plans against Your people, And conspire together against Your treasured ones. They have said, 'Come, and let us wipe them out as a nation, That the name of Israel be remembered no more.' For they have conspired together with one mind; against You they make a covenant.' Psalm 83:1-5

'The land, moreover, shall not be sold permanently, for the land is Mine.' Leviticus 25:23

'A land for which the Lord your God cares; the eyes of the Lord your God are always on it, from the beginning even to the end of the year.' Deuteronomy 11:12

Once the Lord grants a blessing, He does not take it back. Israel remains His chosen people. As Romans 11:29 says, *'For the gifts and calling of God are irrevocable.'*

The Lord will complete His work with the Jews, and His Word does not change. Those promises remain valid today. The Lord tells Amos about a day in which He will restore the captivity of My people Israel, and they will never again be rooted out of their land.

'I will restore the captivity of My people Israel, And they will rebuild the ruined cities and live in them; They will also plant vineyards and drink their wine, And make gardens and eat their fruit. I will also plant them on their land, and they will not again be rooted out from their land which I have given them, Says the Lord your God.' Amos 9:14-15

Firstly, this prophecy is for the Jews and modern day Israel, for the Church has never been in captivity, the Jews have been. Secondly, it must be about modern Israel because the Israelites of the first century were uprooted from their land.

The devil has another purpose in anti-Semitism. The Lord wants to bless people and nations. The word "blessed" is mentioned approximately in Scripture 301 times and "blessing" 73 times (depending on translation). The devil will always try to prevent people from receiving blessings from Jesus. One way is to tempt us to sin and then entice us to run away from the Lord in shame. But another major tactic is to sweep the world with hatred for God's Chosen People. The devil is working to prevent those blessings from becoming a reality in the lives of people. Unfortunately, many in the Church have fallen for the lie of "Replacement Theology", resulting in their failure to receive a greater blessing from the Lord.

Some people hate the Jews because they possess too much wealth and power. Yet, the Jews of East Central Europe over the past 300 years were poor and had no influence. Others have said that the Jews claim to be the Chosen people of G-d.[1] This is viewed as arrogance resulting in rejection of the Jews.

When Germany became a sovereign nation in 1871, many non-observant Jews denied being chosen and married Gentiles. Yet the holocaust started in Germany. Plus, it is interesting to observe how many Christians and Muslims claim to be the chosen people of G-d and do not face persecution.

---

1   The custom of substituting the word "God" with G-d in English is based on the traditional practice in Jewish law of giving God's Hebrew name a high degree of respect and reverence.

For me, I grew up being told that the Jews killed Jesus. Of course as a small child I would believe anything I was told. Today, it is heard in many circles that the Jews rejected Jesus when He was on Earth, so Jesus got mad, rejected the Jews and made the Church the new chosen people. Nevertheless, upon a closer look, the Jews did not reject Jesus outright. The apostles John, Peter, James, Paul, Nicodemus, and many other Jews in the first century followed Jesus Christ. In fact, it could be argued that each person who followed Jesus prior to Cornelius in Acts 10, was Jewish.

On the other hand, the Bible tells us of many Gentiles in the First Century who rejected Jesus and were instrumental in His execution. They include Pilate, King Herod (who was not Jewish but Idumaean), and the Roman officers.

We must cement in our mind that the Jews did not murder Jesus. In fact, if you want to blame anyone – blame me! Jesus died because I have sinned and I am in need of a Savior. In truth, it was our sin that put Christ on the Cross!

It was Replacement Theology in Central Europe in the 18th Century which created a widespread hatred of the Jews. Horrible tales were spread by the Church about Jews mixing blood of Gentile babies into the batter which made Matzos, this infuriated the people. The fact that most Jewish communities were isolated from their neighbors only added to the mystique, fueling false myths. This anti-Semitism created such an atmosphere of hate and distrust of all Jews until it reached its logical conclusion with the Holocaust. Hitler did not create the Holocaust; he merely threw a bit of petrol on the flame which was already burning. The average person in Europe (not only Germany) was eager to participate in the Holocaust because of the foundation laid by Replacement Theology. There were systematic efforts in Spain, Russia, France, Lithuania and England to rid those nations of the Jews long before the Nazis came to power. A difficult book which explains this in detail is, *Hitler's Willing Executioners*, by Daniel Jonah Goldhagen

Let's get rid of any Replacement Theology and walk in the Truth, not in hand-me-down traditions.

You may ask, "How does anti-Semitism and Replacement Theology fit in to a study of strategic spiritual warfare?" We need to remove any hindrances which would stop the blessing of the Lord for us to function properly as the Church. We need the power of the Holy Spirit to enjoy the victories over sin, hell, death, and the world. As we, the Church, bless the Jews, we will experience the blessings Jesus provides.

CHAPTER SIX

The Cross

Perhaps the most powerful strategic event in spiritual warfare is the death of Jesus on the cross. How can an event or action which happened 2000 years ago have real significance today? Jesus gives reference to the defeat of the forces of hell as He speaks of His pending crucifixion.

Jesus said, '*Now judgment is upon this world; now the ruler of this world will be cast out. And I, if I am lifted up from the earth, I will draw all men to Myself.*' John 12:31-32

It was Jesus' death on the Cross which caused the ruler of this world to be cast out.

'*... that through death He might render powerless him who had the power of death, that is the devil, and might free those who through fear of death were subject to slavery all their lives.*' Hebrews 2:14-15

'*For Christ did not send me to baptize, but to preach the gospel, not in cleverness of speech, so that the cross of Christ would not be made void. For the word of the cross is foolishness to those who are perishing, but to us who are being saved it is the power of God. For it is written, "I will destroy the wisdom of the wise, And the cleverness of the clever I will set aside." Where is the wise man? Where is the scribe? Where is the debater of this age? Has not God made foolish the wisdom of the world? For since in the wisdom of God the world through its wisdom did not come to know God, God was well-pleased through the foolishness of the message preached to save those who believe. For indeed Jews ask for signs and Greeks search for wisdom; but we preach Christ crucified, to Jews a stumbling block and to Gentiles foolishness, but to those who are the called, both Jews and Greeks, Christ the power of God and the wisdom of God. Because the foolishness of God is wiser than men, and the weakness of God is stronger than men.'* 1 Corinthians 1:17-25

The cross is foolishness to those who are perishing. Those who do not follow Jesus can only shake their heads at the idea of someone willingly going to a cross. After all, why would someone voluntarily face such agony and shame? The recent movie, *Passion of the Christ*, was criticized in some circles for being too violent. I suspect if we could go back in time and observe; the movie was tame in comparison to actual events. The Bible tells us that Jesus was beaten so badly that He was unrecognizable as a man (Isaiah 52:14). We would see a bloody hunk of mass nailed to the cross. It was also the custom to completely strip the condemned naked. Therefore, they were exposed for all to see. This kind of humiliation, cruelty, shame, and horror could never be adequately expressed in a movie.

The Jews had a visual picture of the Messiah. He would be physically strong and bring political liberation. He would be victorious over all the enemies of God's chosen people. Jesus was the topic of conversation in many places. One example was Nicodemus. In the third chapter of John, he has a secret meeting with Jesus. Nicodemus seems to be telling Jesus something like this, "We have been talking about you over at the Temple. We think you have some type of power and direction from God but we are not sure yet. We are watching and some are even hoping you will rally the people and give us our nation back."

Jesus responds by trying to explain His mission is spiritual not political. The liberation comes to the inner man through a born-again conversion. We should not be critical of Nicodemus for his failure to understand. Nobody understood until after Pentecost.

However, references to the cross are found throughout Scripture. One such passage is Isaiah 52:13 - 53:12 which describes the work of the cross.

'Behold, My servant will prosper, He will be high and lifted up and greatly exalted.' Isaiah 52:13

Jesus was lifted high when on the Cross and then Paul writes in Philippians 2 that the Father highly exalted Him because of His obedience.

'His appearance was marred more than any man and His form more than the sons of men.' Isaiah 52:14

'Surely our griefs He Himself bore, and our sorrows He carried; yet we ourselves esteemed Him stricken, smitten of God, and afflicted. But He was pierced through for our transgressions; He was crushed for our iniquities. The chastening for our well-being fell upon Him, and by His scourging we are healed.' Isaiah 53:4-5

'But the Lord was pleased to crush Him, putting Him to grief. If He would render Himself as a guilt offering, He will see His offspring, He will prolong His days, and the good pleasure of the Lord will prosper in His hand. As a result of the anguish of His soul, He will see it and be satisfied. By His knowledge the Righteous One, My Servant, will justify the many, as He will bear their iniquities. Therefore, I will allot Him a portion with the great. And He will divide the booty with the strong; because He poured out Himself to death, and was numbered with the transgressors. Yet He Himself bore the sin of many, and interceded for the transgressors.' Isaiah 53:10-12

Another look at 1 Corinthians 1:18 shows that while the cross seems foolish to the lost, for Christians, it is the power of God. This is a puzzling statement. How are the gallows the power of God? What was so special about the cross? Paul proceeds in this chapter to contrast the wisdom of the world and the foolishness of God.

Several times in Scripture, God seems to set a trap for the

enemies of His people. For example, Moses was led to the shores of the Red Sea, and the Egyptian army appears to have them trapped. But we know that the Red Sea parted, not only allowing the Israelites to escape into the Sinai, but the Egyptians were drowned when they followed.

Of the many traps set by the Lord, the cross was the biggest trap of all. The wisdom of the world said, "Crucify Jesus and we will get rid of Him forever." But this act of laying down His life was the focal point for all eternity.

It was the cross that made the difference. As singer and song writer, Bill Gaither, penned in 1970:

"*And the old rugged cross made the difference*
In a life bound for heartache and defeat;
I will praise Him forever and ever
For the cross made the difference for me."

Yes indeed, the cross made the difference. It was at the cross that the Power of the Lord was demonstrated. It was at the cross that satan was defeated. The cross is a vital focal point of Christianity and we must always proclaim the cross. Some liberal Christians try to speak only of the love of Jesus and ignore the cross because of the horrid image. Nevertheless, the Cross was the greatest act of love that the world has ever seen. Nobody can speak of the Love of Jesus and ignore His perfect sacrifice at the cross. The cross also shows the awfulness of sin. Sin is terrible. Sin is ugly. Sin destroys. Sin separates us from the love of the Lord, and sin had to be conquered. Sin was conquered at the cross. Look at the cross and see how brutal a sacrifice had to be made so sin would be defeated. At the cross, all can see how the Lord views sin and what desperate measures had to be taken to destroy the power of sin.

'*For it was the Father's good pleasure for all the fullness to dwell in Him (Jesus), and through Him (Jesus) to reconcile all things to Himself, having made peace through the blood of His Cross; through Him, I say, whether things on earth or things in heaven. And although you were formerly alienated and hostile in mind, engaged in evil deeds, yet He has now reconciled you in His fleshly body through death, in order to present you before Him holy and blameless and beyond reproach.'* Colossians 1:19-22

The importance of Christian unity in revival and spiritual warfare will be discussed in a later chapter. The key to unity is reconciliation. At the cross, Jesus provided the means for man to be reconciled to God. Jesus paved the way so we could achieve forgiveness for our sins. The gap between God and man which existed because of sin had been breached by the blood of Jesus on the Cross.

As Christians receive forgiveness of sins and the new-found relationship with our Heavenly Father, we are now in a position through the Holy Spirit to achieve reconciliation with each other. Reconciliation is such a powerful weapon of our warfare that an entire chapter of this book is devoted to an examination of it.

Again, the power of the cross is demonstrated as Paul writes about being dead in our transgressions, but now we are alive together with Him (Jesus) because we have been totally forgiven.

'*When you were dead in transgressions and the uncircumcision of your flesh, He made you alive together with Him, having forgiven us all our transgressions, having cancelled out the certificate of debt consisting of decrees against us, which was hostile to us; and He has taken it out of the way, having nailed it to the Cross.'* Colossians 2:13-15

Our sins are like a certificate of debt which He has taken away from us and nailed to the Cross. Imagine someone having an official document saying that you are in such heavy debt that all the money in the world could never pay it off. Then imagine a wealthy benefactor paying the debt from another world (Heaven) with unlimited resources. They stamp your document PAID IN FULL!

In the same way, our sins were nailed on the cross and Jesus paid the debt. When He cried, "It is finished!" (John 19:30), Jesus was literally saying, "It is paid for."

Our debt has been totally and completely paid. All those who put their faith and trust in Jesus are now forgiven. The certificate of debt was nailed to the Cross.

The devil was the accuser of the brethren until he got thrown out of Heaven. (Revelation 12:10) But his nature is still the accuser. The only difference is that he whispers accusations if you listen to him. There is a difference between just words and having power. Colossians 2:15 states,

'When He (Jesus) had disarmed the rulers and authorities, He made a public display of them, having triumphed over them through Him.'

In the days of the Roman Empire, conquerors returned to Rome after their military victories, with the vanquished on parade in chains. In like manner, all the hosts of hell have been put on display in the Heavenly realms, to show all with spiritual awareness of the defeat of the devil. It is therefore vital to live in the victory Jesus provides.

Certainly, if the cross caused the devil to be publicly displayed as a defeated foe, then our use of the cross will bring continued victory. As we use the cross, it brings a spiritual presence which binds the forces of darkness.

Today there are attempts made to prevent Christians from displaying the cross. Some who wear a necklace with a cross are told it is offensive and that they cannot wear such jewelry at their workplace. Others are told that a small cross on display on their desk must be removed or their jobs may be in jeopardy. Why is the mere presence of a small cross causing so much controversy? It is because the cross is a spiritual weapon of warfare. The devil and demons shake at its presence. The devil inspires his followers to rise up in anger and demand that all symbols of Christianity be removed from public view.

There are many Christians who are fearful of public outreach, but one outreach you can do is to engage in strategic spiritual warfare by simply displaying a cross.

'He (Jesus) Himself bore our sins in His body on the Cross, so that we might die to sin and live to righteousness.' 1 Peter 2:24

The apostle Peter tells the Church that the cross provides the power we have: we need to live righteously as righteousness is another weapon of strategic spiritual warfare which we will examine further.

The Cross at Rephidim

The cross provides more than righteousness, it has been a sign of encouragement for thousands of years.

'Then Amalek came and fought against Israel at Rephidim. So Moses said to Joshua, 'Choose men for us and go out, fight against Amalek. Tomorrow I will station myself on the top of the hill with the staff of God in my hand.' Joshua did as Moses told him, and fought against Amalek; and Moses, Aaron, and Hur went up to the top of the hill. So it came about when Moses held his hand up, that Israel prevailed, and when he let his hand down, Amalek prevailed. But Moses' hands were heavy. Then they took a stone and put it under him, and he sat on it; and Aaron and Hur supported his hands, one on one side and one on the other. Thus his hands were steady until the sun set. So Joshua overwhelmed Amalek and his people with the edge of the sword.' Exodus 17:8-13

Looking up from the battlefield, Joshua would have seen Moses standing with outstretched arms which would have looked like a cross. Even before Jesus was born in Bethlehem, the cross was a sign of victory.

Jesus Endured the Cross for Joy

This Scripture is both powerful yet puzzling.

'Therefore, since we have so great a cloud of witnesses surrounding us, let us also lay aside every encumbrance and the sin which so easily entangles us, and let us run with endurance the race that is set before us, fixing our eyes on Jesus, the author and perfecter of faith, who for the joy set before Him endured the cross, despising the shame, and has sat down at the right hand of the throne of God.' Hebrews 12:1-2

Crucifixion is the most horrible experience anyone could suffer. While Jesus suffered the physical pain, the humiliation of not only the jeering crowd but being exposed naked for everyone to see; the biggest heartache for our Lord was the separation from His Father. He cried, *"Eloi, Eloi, Lama Sabachthani" which is translated "My God, My God, why have you forsaken Me?"* (Mark 15:34) Yet Jesus endured the Cross with joy.

Our Holy Heavenly Father cannot look at sin, and when Jesus was on the cross, He became the sin of the world. For the only time from eternity past to eternity future, the relationship between Father and Son was broken. This pain of this broken relationship was more agonizing than any human being will ever fully comprehend. The writer of Hebrews explains that Jesus endured the cross for the joy set before Him. What was the joy?

The joy was seeing relationships build between sinful man and His Father. The joy was seeing the power of sin destroyed. The joy was seeing lives restored through forgiveness and love. The joy was seeing the defeat of the devil. For Jesus, this joy made the cross worth all the pain, suffering, and shame.

We as Christians need to understand the cross and the victory achieved on the cross. We need to see the cross as a sign of this victory and as a great weapon to be used in our spiritual warfare.

The devil knows how the cross is so powerful, to the point that even some churches will not allow a cross in their sanctuaries. Their excuse is, Catholics have a cross. This demonstrates ignorance, for technically the Catholics do not have a cross; they have a crucifix, which is the cross with Jesus on the cross. Yet we know that He is no longer on the cross, therefore, let us not be ashamed to present the cross!

Carrying the Cross

One strategic spiritual warrior who needs to be acknowledged is Arthur Blessett. I had the joy of spending a day with Arthur in Belfast as we carried crosses side by side. Arthur shared with us how he grew up in Mississippi and then moved to Southern California in the "hippie days of the 60's." There he would proclaim that we needed to get high on Jesus rather than on drugs. Arthur is very outgoing (to put it mildly) and is very bold in his public witness. He was, and still is unorthodox in many ways.

One day, while in prayer, as he was looking at a large cross hanging on the wall in his sanctuary, the Lord told him to take it down and carry it across town. Arthur Blessett obeyed. Then the Lord told him to carry it across the country. So began, a worldwide adventure of carrying the cross.

Arthur claims to have carried the Cross in almost every nation. One such adventure was to carry the cross from the northernmost point of North America, through Central America, and to the southernmost point in South America. Some might say it is a publicity stunt, but look deeper; it is an act of strategic spiritual warfare. Even in the jungles of Central America, where nobody is looking, as he carried the Cross, the message of the Cross was being proclaimed into the Heavenly realm.

Arthur has worn out several Crosses in his journeys. The one he uses today has wheels so that it will last longer. His first cross was destroyed as it was dragged along the road. Today, his cross is collapsible so he can pack it in a suitcase to carry on airplanes as he travels around the world.

Arthur Blessett has a most interesting story. Consequently, the essential point is: Arthur has been on a worldwide crusade presenting the Cross to everyone he can. Needless to say, a man coming down the street carrying a ten-foot Cross is going to get some attention. Because of his bold and outgoing personality, he is able to speak personally with hundreds of people each day.

Another example of carrying the Cross was by a pastor in Belfast, Northern Ireland. Pastor Jack McKee carried the Cross in 2002 through the paramilitary areas of both Catholic and Protestant sections, where gun and bomb had ruled. Again this act was a prayer effort to bring the power of the cross into his community. The cross had "John 3:16" in bold letters across the beam. He would often be asked, "What is John 3:16?"

Then in 2009, for 40 days, Jack stood holding a cross between noon and 3pm at the Peace Wall in Belfast separating The Shankill and The Falls. Between 1970 and 1997, The Shankill and The Falls saw terrible tragedy, destruction, and murder during "The Troubles", as warring factions brought havoc on each other's communities. In many ways, Jack's "See you at the Cross" became the talk of the town.

Today the New Life City church stands next to the peace line and at the spot where Jack did his forty day stand. They have a vibrant ministry with The Shankill (Loyalist/Protestant) and The Falls (Nationalist/Catholic). Many broken people have met the healer and savior in Jesus Christ. The spiritual foundation of this congregation can be traced back to the cross events. The Holy Spirit was unleashed and the powers of darkness were bound. On a regular basis Jack McKee[2] and New Life City Church continue what Jack now calls, "C U at the Cross" events. It is a simple yet powerful demonstration presenting the Cross to the community and praying for the Gospel to manifest.

There is more about "C U at the Cross" in the final chapter, in which methods of strategic spiritual warfare are explained, so that local congregations can be active with special events.

---

2   Jack McKee's & New Life City church story is told in full in
        'What does it take?' published by Maurice Wylie Media.

CHAPTER 7

The Word

Perhaps the most important weapon a Christian has is their Bible. The Bible is not meant to simply be a devotion book, nor a textbook, but a living active power available for every Christian to change lives and the world.

I want to begin this chapter with a group of Scriptures about "The Word" of God – the Bible!

'In the beginning was the Word, and the Word was with God, and the Word was God.' John 1:1

'All things came into being through Him (The Word), and apart from Him nothing came into being that has come into being. In Him was life, and the life was the Light of men.' John 1:3-4

'And the Word became flesh, and dwelt among us, and we saw His glory, glory as of the only begotten from the Father, full of grace and truth.' John 1:14

'But as many as received Him (The Word), to them He gave the right to become children of God, even to those who believe in His name.' John 1:12

'For the Word of God is living and active and sharper than any two-edged sword, and piercing as far as the division of the soul and

spirit, of both joints and marrow, and able to judge the thoughts and intentions of the heart.' Hebrews 4:12

'Is not My Word like fire?' declares the LORD, 'and like a hammer which shatters a rock?' Jeremiah 23:29

'Heaven and earth will pass away, but My Words will not pass away.' Matthew 24:35

'If you continue in My Word, then you are truly disciples of Mine; and you will know the truth, and the truth will make you free.' John 8:31-32

'All Scripture is inspired by God and profitable for teaching, for reproof, for correction, for training in righteousness; so that the man of God may be adequate, equipped for every good work.' 2 Timothy 3:16-17

'for you have been born again... through the living and enduring word of God.' 1 Peter 1:23

In Mark Chapter 4 we read of the Parable of the Sower. The sower sows seed in four different places. When Jesus gives the explanation of the parable, He says that the sower sows the Word and the good soil produces a thirty, sixty, and a hundredfold harvest. This parable teaches that it is the Word which multiplies and it is the Word which enters the hearts of men to accomplish the will and purposes of the Lord.

'And He said to them, 'Do you not understand this parable?' How will you understand all the parables?' Mark 4:13

Jesus informs His followers about the importance of this parable. Unless the Parable of the Sower is understood, the others will not be understood, because this is the most important parable. The Word is sown in our hearts and it is the Word which gives understanding. Without a good and healthy knowledge of the Word, nobody will be able to understand the Kingdom of Heaven or produce fruit. The Word sown into hearts is the foundation of the Church.

In the realm of spiritual warfare, the Parable of the Sower also gives us the enemy of the Word: hard hearts, affliction, persecution, worries of the world, and deceitfulness of riches. It is the proper use of the Word which defeats our spiritual enemies.

The Word is Under Attack

In the Garden of Eden, the devil questioned Eve by challenging the Word God gave her. The devil implied to her, "You can eat the forbidden fruit, God has lied to you."

The Philosopher Voltaire (1694-1778) is reported to have said 100 years after his death; the Bible will disappear from the face of the Earth. In 1878, his house in Geneva, Switzerland, was the home of *The Geneva Bible society*.

In more modern times, Josh McDowell became a Christian because of his study to disprove it. He was challenged by a group of Christians at his university. They kept telling him, "Jesus loves you." He got angry and took time to study about the Bible for the express purpose of disproving it. At the conclusion of his study, he reached the decision that not only the Bible is true; but it is true that Jesus loves him. He became a Christian by his study of the Word. His testimony is given in his tape series, *Belief Matters*.

Another man named Mustafa was given the task of revealing the distortions of the Christian faith. As he studied the Bible, he reached the conclusion that the Bible is true and that Jesus is the Savior of the world. His story is told in the book, *Secret Believers*, by Brother Andrew.

The Word

'And the Word became flesh, and dwelt among us, and we saw His glory, glory, as of the only begotten from the Father, full of grace and truth.' John 1:14

God the Father manifested the Word of God to us as the Saviour Jesus Christ.

Jesus said to him, 'I am the way, and the truth, and the Life...' John 14:6 What was Jesus saying? He was saying that the Word is the Way, is Truth and has Life.

In John 8:42-45 it describes a conversation with Pharisees. Jesus accused them of following their father, the devil. Can you remember what the devil is? He is a liar and the father of lies. He has no truth!

Our weapon to combat lies is Truth. So, can I ask you a question? Is there any part of your life in which you are living a lie? Is there any part of your storyline in which you feel the need to lie, even to God? My friend, to be free from the workings of the devil we MUST depart from his evil ways and live in Truth to ourselves and the Word of God.

As Scripture says, '...*The Son of God appeared for this purpose, to destroy the works of the devil.'* 1 John 3:8

When the devil comes to tempt, remember that Jesus used the Word when tempted in the wilderness (Matthew 4:1-13). You and I as Christians have the authority to use the Word in our spiritual battles.

Scripture tells us how effective the Word is: '*For the word of God is living and active and sharper than any two-edged sword, and piercing as far as the division of soul and spirit, of both joints and marrow, and quick to judge the thoughts and intentions of the heart.'* Hebrews 4:12

We, as Christians, need to be trained warriors of the Kingdom, not just pew fodder, programmed to think that the Church is a building. Yet, Jesus never died for a building but for hearts of the people.

We have built a generation of believers that at trained to attend church but not be the Church. Millions of dollars/pounds are spent on buildings that are locked up, empty of God's presence, and congregations taught to be dependent on a building or a pastor, rather than God's voice and His presence. How far have we the Church fallen? We wonder why the "gates of hell" does prevail when Scripture states the opposite? Could it be that something is not right?

It would seem the chief objective of many in the church is to stay safe. Safety is more important than victory. Worse yet, many times we ignore the enemy and simply do nothing. Strategic spiritual warfare is always offensive. We take the initiative, we take the fight to the enemy's camp. If we are going to be effective in our Christianity - we need to be Kingdom warriors!

'So will My word be which goes forth from My mouth; It will not return to Me empty, Without accomplishing what I desire, And without succeeding in the matter for which I sent it.' Isaiah 55:11

'For the word of God is living and active and sharper than any two-edged sword...' Hebrews 4:12

What a great unconditional promise from the Lord! The Word is sharper than a two edge sword, cutting as it goes in and out that His Word will accomplish the purposes of the Lord and can only be fruitful. It is the Word that will bring the Kingdom of Heaven onto the earth. This is a Scripture that the Church needs to read, meditate on, preach, proclaim, and believe. It demonstrates the power of the Word.

It is the Word which will give us victory over the powers of darkness and is a huge weapon in our strategic spiritual warfare.

'He (Jesus) is clothed with a robe dipped in blood, and His name is called The Word of God.' Revelation 19:13

How can we best use this weapon?

A. Proclaim the Word.

In February 2012, I was able to enter North Korea. I knew I would only be there for a short time so in order to make the most of it, I wanted to proclaim the Word of God. Psalm 86:9 was a good verse to claim and proclaim to the people of North Korea. *"All nations whom You have made shall come and worship before You, O Lord. And they shall glorify Your Name."*

This practice was made real to me in 2010 while on a prayer journey through the "Silk Road." Our team flew to Beijing, China and traveled overland to Istanbul, Turkey. We would take our Bibles and go to mountain tops overlooking large cities. Other days we would be on trains traveling through the county side. As we looked at China, Kazakhstan and the other nations, we would take the promises from the Bible and proclaim its truth to the people and the land.

Jesus spoke words of life. We have the privilege of speaking those same words of Scripture to bring life into our world. Proclaiming Light into darkness - the light of the Word

We were claiming China in the Name of Jesus for the Kingdom of Heaven. We had faith the promises of Scripture would become a reality for the Chinese people. Some Scriptures we used are below. Imagine as you read these passages, the power of Jesus flowing over China. And then, in the same way, proclaim them afresh over your city and your nation.

'O dry bones, hear the word of the Lord... I will cause breath to enter you that you may come to life.' Ezekiel 37:4

'...the words that I have spoken to you are spirit and are life.' John 6:63

'But you are a chosen race, a royal priesthood, a holy nation,

a people for God's own possession, so that you may proclaim the excellences of Him who has called you out of darkness into His marvellous light.' 1 Peter 2:9

'O afflicted one, storm-tossed, and not comforted, Behold, I will set your stones in antimony, And your foundations I will lay in sapphires. Moreover, I will make your battlements of rubies, And your gates of crystal, And your entire wall of precious stones. All your sons will be taught of the LORD; AND THE WELL-BEING OF YOUR SONS WILL BE GREAT. In righteousness you will be established; You will be far from oppression, for you will not fear; And from terror, for it will not come near you.' Isaiah 54:11-14

'At one moment I might speak concerning a nation or concerning a kingdom to uproot, to pull down, or to destroy it; if that nation against which I have spoken turns from its evil, I will relent concerning the calamity I planned to bring on it. Or at another moment I might speak concerning a nation or concerning a kingdom to build up or to plant it; if it does evil in My sight by not obeying My voice, then I will think better of the good with which I had promised to bless it. So now then, speak to the men of Judah and against the inhabitants of Jerusalem saying, 'Thus says the LORD, 'BEHOLD, I AM FASHIONING CALAMITY AGAINST YOU AND DEVISING A PLAN AGAINST YOU. OH TURN BACK, EACH OF YOU FROM HIS EVIL WAY, AND REFORM YOUR WAYS AND YOUR DEEDS.' Jeremiah 18:7-11

B. Bible reading marathons

The Bible can be read orally from cover to cover in about 80 hours. When a group reads the entire Bible in a marathon; the Holy Spirit moves with power.

1. Brings people together - unity

2. Proclaims the Word into the spiritual realm.

3. Gives many a new appreciation for the Bible and a desire to read it for themselves.

As the Word is proclaimed out loud in its entirety, principalities and powers of darkness are threatened. When I was living in Belfast, Northern Ireland, our Bible reading marathon resulted in many salvations and moves of peace in the neighborhood. More is written about our Bible reading marathon in the last chapter, where we will look at practical ways that local churches and fellowship can engage in strategic spiritual warfare.

C. Read/Study entire books at once.

I would suggest that there are times when a book of the Bible is read completely without stopping to comment. This is a neat way for a small group to have Bible study. It should be a short book and there could be teaching and discussion following the reading. But there is much to be gained by reading an entire book out loud allowing the Holy Spirit to teach and exhort.

A smaller book such as Paul's letter to the Ephesians could be read and discussed in an hour. Other books such as Revelation could be the topic of a Saturday meeting. Revelation can be read in about an hour and a half. Then a discussion can follow. Hopefully, participants in this kind of Bible study would become more interested in further study, as whole books are presented instead of simply a few verses which may be taken out of context.

D. Know the Word

Jesus overcame temptation in Matthew 4 because He knew and answered with Scripture. To live in victory, we must have the ability to recognize temptation and then answer it with Scripture. Knowing the Word is essential for this victory. Our dedication to learn the Word is necessary as well. Knowing the Word takes time and effort, and to have humility will allow us to ask a mature Christian about passages and verses not understood.

Also, an understandable translation is best, and in an era when the Internet is so available, online Bible translations are readily accessible.

E. Use the Word to encourage others.

Romans 8 is an example of encouraging passages. Let us look at this chapter.

v1 – *'Therefore there is now no condemnation for those who are in Christ Jesus.'*

v11 – *'If the Spirit of Him who raised Jesus from the dead dwells in you, He who raised Christ Jesus from the dead will also give life to your mortal bodies through His Spirit who dwells in you.'*

v18 – *'For I consider that the sufferings of this present time are not worthy to be compared with the glory that is to be revealed to us.'*

v28 – *'And we know that God causes all things to work together for good to those who love God, to those who are called according to His purpose.'*

v35 – *'Who will separate us from the love of Christ? Will tribulation, or distress, or persecution, or famine, or nakedness, or peril, or sword?'*

v37-39 – *'But in all these things we overwhelmingly conquer through Him who loved us.* (Conquer is a battlefield term - it means winning the battle) *For I am convinced that neither death, nor life, nor angels, nor principalities, nor things present, nor things to come, nor powers, nor height, nor depth, nor any other created thing, will be able to separate us from the love of God, which is in Christ Jesus our Lord.'*

This look at Romans 8 is not to preach, but to encourage. This is only one example of how The Word is a powerful weapon to bring hope and energy to our Christian life. While the powers of darkness want to create fear and confusion, the Word brings life and encouragement. We are fully equipped to engage in joyfully living out the Christian life.

F. If Jesus used the Word when He was tempted, we certainly cannot expect to have victory without it.

There is a danger when studying the Word of God to treat it as an intellectual exercise. The Word has a lot of mysteries but remember they are there to be uncovered. We can all have questions about the Bible but it is no different than having questions about life: "How did that happen?" "Who are they?" Many times, I would ponder over the "wise men" who visited the infant Jesus? How many were there? I know most churches teach that there were 3 wise men but Scripture does not state that. What it does state is that there were 3 types of gifts that they brought; gold (gift for a king), frankincense (gift for a god), and myrrh (gift for death). It is important that in learning a truth that it is Truth to start with.

Leaders

One can make an argument that the main contribution of the United States in the Allied victory during World War II was not in military might but in industrial might. Often figures such as General Dwight Eisenhower, General George Patton, General Douglas MacArthur, Admiral Chester Nimitz, and General George Marshall are featured in historical accounts of World War II. However, perhaps it was Andrew Higgins who did more to win the war than any of the above. But who was Andrew Higgins?

President Dwight Eisenhower stated that Andrew Higgins was the man who won the war for the USA. Andrew Higgins was in the lumber business and lived in the swamps of Louisiana. He invented and built a boat which could travel in the shallow water in search of trees to use as lumber. These boats were mass produced and used as landing craft for the invasion of Normandy on 6th June 1944, as well as numerous other assaults from the sea. Higgins Industries produced over 20,000 boats used in both European and Pacific theaters of the war.

The Holy Spirit gives the Church and each individual Christian strategic superiority as well. Our prayers for leaders, missionaries, and our brothers/sisters suffering for their faith, will energize Heavenly power to fulfill the purposes of Christ and build His

Church. Revelation 5:8 states that the prayers of the Saints are stored in Heaven. Just as the production of the industries in the United States developed powerful resources which defeated immense foes, our continual prayers against spiritual forces of wickedness will result in victory for the Kingdom of Heaven to the glory of Jesus Christ our Lord. Just as the superiority of the industrial production provided the means for Allied victory in World War II, our prayer production will be the means for victory in Jesus.

CHAPTER 8

The Name of Jesus

The Name of Jesus is another divinely powerful weapon given to us in our strategic spiritual warfare.

Acts chapter 3 tells us a wonderful story about how the Name of Jesus was used to bring healing and wholeness to a forty-year-old crippled beggar. Peter and John were entering the Temple when this man who had been there every day for no telling how long, asked them for money. Peter and John had something better than money to provide, a life changing experience for the beggar. They had the Name of Jesus as a weapon of spiritual warfare and they used this divinely powerful weapon to change not only this man's life but 5,000 others who came to know the Lord before the sun set.

Why would the Name of Jesus bring power into our situation? One simple explanation would be to examine Matthew 1, where the angel comes to Joseph after he learns Mary is expecting a child.

'She (Mary) will bear a Son; and you shall call His Name Jesus, for He will save His people from their sins.' Matthew 1:21

The angel reveals the Child Mary is carrying was conceived by the Holy Spirit and His name would be Jesus, translated as, "God with us." As we proclaim the Name Jesus, as we use the Name Jesus against the powers of darkness; we are calling upon Him who is with us and eager to make His presence known for His glory.

Jesus told us to use His Name and it seems to me, this implies that we are given authority by using His Name to impact worldly circumstances. It can be compared to using "For the Commander" in a military document. When I was in the Army, many staff officers would write directives. The power of the directive came from these three little words at the bottom: "For the Commander." In other words, this directive is not really from a Captain or Lieutenant, but it has the power of the Colonel who commands the Brigade.

The prayers of Christians like you and me can flow into the Heavenly places with the power of Jesus Christ Himself. The only conditions I see are that we must use the Name of Jesus and pray according to His will and purpose.

A Bible study of the Name of Jesus will bring encouragement to our spirits because the Bible is filled with examples of how the Name of Jesus brings power, purpose, protection, and provision. In this chapter, I feel the need to share many Scriptures which tell of the power in the Name of Jesus. The Word can speak for itself.

On the day of Pentecost, the early Church proclaimed the Name of Jesus to demonstrate the power in the Name, and we need to be doing it again.

'Peter said to them, Repent, and each of you be baptized in the Name of Jesus Christ for the forgiveness of your sins; and you will receive the gift of the Holy Spirit.' Acts 2:38

"In the Name of Jesus Christ the Nazarene – Walk!" Acts 3:6

'And on the basis of faith in His name, it is the name of Jesus which has strengthened this man whom you see and know; and the faith which comes through Him has given him this perfect health in the presence of you all.' Acts 3:16

'let it be known to all of you and to all the people of Israel, by the

name of Jesus Christ the Nazarene, whom you crucified, whom God raised from the dead – by this name this man stands here before you in good health.' Acts 4:10

'And there is salvation in no one else; for there is no other name under heaven that has been given among men by which we must be saved.' Acts 4:12

'But so that it will not spread any further among the people, let us warn them to speak no longer to any man in this Name. And when they had summoned them, they commanded them not to speak or teach at all in the name of Jesus.' Acts 4:17-18

In the book of John, Chapters 14-16, the term "in My name" is used seven times.

'Whatever you ask in My name, that I will do, so that the Father may be glorified in the Son.' John 14:13

'If you ask Me anything in My name, I will do it.' John 14:14

'But the Helper, the Holy Spirit, whom the Father will send in My name, He will teach you all things, and bring to your remembrance all that I said to you.' John 14:26

'You did not choose Me but I chose you, and appointed you that you would go and bear fruit, and that your fruit would remain, so that whatever you ask of the Father in My name He may give to you.' John 15:16

'But all these things they will do to you for My name's sake, because they do not know the One who sent Me.' John 15:21

'...Truly, truly, I say to you, if you ask the Father for anything in My name, He will give it to you. Until now you have asked for nothing in My name; ask and you will receive, so that our joy may be made full.' John 16:23-24

'In that day you will ask in My name, and I do not say to you that I will request of the Father on your behalf.' John 16:26

The John 16:26 passage explains why many Christians end their prayers with "in Jesus Name." Our petitions have been asked in Jesus Name.

'Therefore many other signs Jesus also performed in the presence of the disciples, which are not written in this book; but these have been written so that you may believe that Jesus is the Christ, the Son of God; and that believing you may have life in His name.' John 20:30-31

Even Proverbs known as the book of wisdom tells us:

'The name of the LORD is a strong tower; The righteous runs into it and is safe.' Proverbs 18:10

Acts 16:18 - Paul used the Name of Jesus to cast the demon out of the slave girl of the fortune tellers. This resulted in their imprisonment in the Philippian jail.

Paul gives his testimony to King Agrippa in Acts 26. Paul tells of his desire to destroy anything which had to do with the Name of Jesus prior to his personal encounter with Christ.

'So then, I (Paul) thought to myself that I had to do many things hostile to the name of Jesus of Nazareth.' Acts 26:9

Paul gives us a preview of Heaven and how everyone who ever existed will participate in a huge worship moment. This is likely before judgment and the lost are sent to hell. Before they depart, they will bow their knee at the Name of Jesus.

'So at the name of Jesus every knee will bow, of those who are in heaven and on earth and under the earth, and that every tongue will confess that Jesus Christ is Lord, to the glory of God the Father.' Philippians 2:10-11

'To the church of God which is at Corinth, to those who have been sanctified in Christ Jesus, saints by calling, with all who in every place call on the name of our Lord Jesus Christ, their Lord and ours.' 1Corinthians 1:2

'the seventy returned with joy, saying 'Lord, even the demons are subject to us in Your name.' Luke 10:17

The Name of Jesus is essential for salvation.

'Whoever will call on the Name of the Lord will be saved.' Romans 10:13 and Joel 2:32

'For from the rising of the sun even to its setting, My name will be great among the nations, and in every place incense is going to be offered to My name, and a grain offering that is pure; for my Name will be great among the nations, says the Lord of hosts.' Malachi 1:11

'Is anyone among you sick? Let him call for the elders of the Church, and let them pray over him, anointing him with oil in the Name of the Lord.' James 5:14

Praying in Jesus' name means praying according to God's will. Praying in Jesus' Name is praying for things which will honor and glorify Jesus.

'This is the confidence which we have before Him, that, if we ask anything according to His will, He hears us. And if we know that he hears us in whatever we ask, we know that we have the requests which we have asked from Him.' 1 John 5:14-15

Years ago, I was active in a denomination who are a wonderful group of Christians, and I enjoyed my time in fellowship and ministry with them.

However, when I was seeking a license to preach with them, I met with a group of pastors for an interview. One question concerned Baptism. I answered the question saying Biblical Baptism was by immersion and quoted Matthew 28:19 and Acts 2:38.

'Go therefore and make disciples of all nations, baptizing them in the name of the Father and the Son and the Holy Spirit.' Matthew 28:19

'Peter said to them, 'Repent, and each of you be baptized in the

name of Jesus Christ for the forgiveness of your sins; and you will receive the gift of the Holy Spirit.' Acts 2:38

I vividly remember them patiently explaining how important it was to use the term "I baptize you in the Name of the Father, the Son and the Holy Spirit" and do not use the term, "In Jesus name." They helped me revise my application form to exclude the Acts 2:38 Scripture.

At the time, I did not pay much attention to it as I was grateful that they were helping me to answer the questions properly for those who made the decision to approve my application. However, looking back today, it is sad that there is any debate such as this at all. After all, if the early Church was encouraged to use the Name of Jesus, surely wisdom would say the same for today.

One example is in Acts, Peter was asked what power or what name have you provided for healing the lame man who was begging at the Temple. As part of his explanation, Peter proclaimed:

'And there is salvation in no one else; for there is no other name under heaven that has been given among men by which we must be saved.' Acts 4:12

As we continue to use the Name of Jesus in prayer and in proclaiming His purposes, we are attacking the spiritual forces of darkness and wickedness, binding their power and thwarting their evil plans. Change is waiting to happen when we use the Name of Jesus!

CHAPTER 9

The Blood

Why is the Church so scared of talking about the blood of Jesus? Especially when the word "blood" occurs over 400 times in the Bible. This tells us that it must be very important to the Kingdom of Heaven.

'Moreover, they shall take some of the blood and put it on the two doorposts and on the lintel of the houses in which they eat it.' Exodus 12:7

'The blood shall be a sign for you on the houses where you live; and when I see the blood I will pass over you, and no plague will befall you to destroy you when I strike the land of Egypt.' Exodus 12:13

'You shall take a bunch of hyssop and dip it in the blood which is in the basin, and apply some of the blood that is in the basin to the lintel and the two doorposts; and none of you shall go outside the door of his house until morning. For the LORD WILL PASS THROUGH TO SMITE THE EGYPTIANS; AND WHEN HE SEES THE BLOOD ON THE LINTEL AND ON THE TWO DOORPOSTS, THE LORD WILL PASS OVER THE DOOR AND WILL NOT ALLOW THE DESTROYER TO COME IN TO YOUR HOUSES TO SMITE YOU.' Exodus 12:22-23

'But when Christ appeared as a high priest of the good things to come, He entered through the greater and more perfect tabernacle, not

made with hands, that is to say, not of this creation; and not through the blood of goats and calves, but through His own blood, He entered the holy place once for all, having obtained eternal redemption. For if the blood of goats and bulls and the ashes of a heifer sprinkling those who have been defiled sanctify for the cleansing of the flesh, how much more will the blood of Christ, who through the eternal Spirit offered Himself without blemish to God, cleanse your conscience from dead works to serve the living God?' Hebrews 9:11-14

When I think of this door, with blood at the top and more blood on the right-hand side and the left-hand side, it makes me think of the cross. The crown of thorns Jesus wore and the nails driven into His hands are symbolized by the specific placement of blood on the door.

In the Old Testament, God many times told His people that the sacrificial system of the Temple was not perfect and there would someday come a perfect sacrifice.

Whereas the blood of the Passover lamb gave only temporary forgiveness of sins, for it covered the sin. This perfect sacrifice came through the blood of Jesus and would not just cover our sin but remove it. Similarly, while the blood of the Passover lamb in Egypt gave temporary protection, the blood of Jesus gives permanent protection, provided we meet the conditions.

'What are your multiplied sacrifices to Me?' Says the Lord. 'I have had enough of burnt offerings of rams and the fat of fed cattle; and I take no pleasure in the blood of bulls, lambs or goats.' Isaiah 1:11

The cup in Communion is a symbol of the blood of Jesus shed for the forgiveness of sins. Communion is a sacrament which is another weapon discussed in the chapter on sacraments.

'For this is My blood of the covenant, which is poured out for many for forgiveness of sins.' Matthew 26:28

'And all the people said, His blood shall be on us and on our children.' Matthew 27:25

Seven Truths About the Blood of Jesus

1. The blood of Jesus provides life not death. Leviticus 17:11 tells us *"life is in the blood."* As Christians plead the blood of Jesus within the Will of the Lord, we will gain victory.

'So Jesus said to them, 'Truly, truly, I say to you, unless you eat the flesh of the Son of Man and drink His blood, you have no life in yourselves. He who eats My flesh and drinks My blood has eternal life, and I will raise him up on the last day. For My flesh is true food, and My blood is true drink. He who eats My flesh and drinks My blood abides in Me, and I in him.' John 6:53-56

2. The blood of Jesus provides forgiveness not condemnation.

'In Him we have redemption through His blood, the forgiveness of our trespasses, according to the riches of His grace.' Ephesians 1:7

'whom God displayed publicly as a propitiation in His blood through faith. This was to demonstrate His righteousness, because in the forbearance of God He passed over the sins previously committed.' Romans 3:25

3. The blood of Jesus provides redemption (we were purchased by His blood) not rejection. We have fellowship with our Heavenly Father.

'Be on guard for yourselves and for all the flock, among which the Holy Spirit has made you overseers, to shepherd the church of God which He purchased with His own blood.' Acts 20:28

'Knowing that you were not redeemed with perishable things like silver or gold from your futile way of life inherited from your forefather, but with precious blood, as of a lamb unblemished and spotless, the blood of Christ.' 1 Peter 1:18-19

'But if we walk in the Light as He Himself is in the Light, we have fellowship with one another, and the blood of Jesus His Son cleanses us from all sin.' 1 John 1:7

'And they sang a new song, saying, 'Worthy are You to take the book and to break its seals; for You were slain, and purchased for God with Your blood men from every tribe and tongue and people and nation.' Revelation 5:9

4   The blood of Jesus provides reconciliation not strife.

'And through Him to reconcile all things to Himself, having made peace through the blood of His cross; through Him, I say, whether things on earth or things in heaven.' Colossians 1:20

'Much more then, having now been justified by His blood, we shall be saved from the wrath of God through Him.' Romans 5:9

'But now in Christ Jesus you who formerly were far off have been brought near by the blood of Christ.' Ephesians 2:13

5. The blood of Jesus provides cleansing, and takes away our shame.

'But into the second, only the high priest enters once a year, not without taking blood, which he offers for himself and for the sins of the people committed in ignorance.' Hebrews 9:7

Other Scriptural references: Hebrews 9:12-14, Hebrews 9:18-25, Hebrews 10:19

6. The blood of Jesus provides sanctification, not bondage to sin.

'For the bodies of those animals whose blood is brought into the holy place by the high priest as an offering for sin, are burned outside the camp. Therefore Jesus also, that He might sanctify the people through His own blood, suffered outside the gate.' Hebrews 13:11-12

'I said to him, 'My lord, you know,' And he said to me, 'These are the ones who come out of the great tribulation, and they have washed their robes and made them white in the blood of the Lamb.' Revelation 7:14

7. The blood of Jesus provides victory over the devil, not defeat by the hands of the devil.

'*Then I heard a loud voice in heaven, saying, 'Now the salvation, and the power, and the kingdom of our God and the authority of His Christ have come, for the accuser of our brethren has been thrown down, he who accuses them before our God day and night. And they overcame him because of the blood of the Lamb and because of the word of their testimony, and they did not love their life even when faced with death.*' Revelation 12:10-11

Revelation 12:11 teaches that we overcome the devil by the blood of the Lamb, which is the ultimate in strategic spiritual attack on the devil. It is wonderful news that we can overcome the darkness which can surround, but we need to meet the 'terms of the contract', to overcome. While the blood of Jesus overcomes our accuser, there are two conditional elements: The word of our testimony; we do not love our lives even when faced with death. As we proclaim the goodness of Jesus, our focus is on what Christ has done, not what the devil is doing – change of focus will help you overcome. The other condition is more drastic, we must love Jesus more than our own lives. We must be prepared to sacrifice our lives rather than compromise. As long as we continue to put self first, we will never have spiritual maturity of an overcomer. There is only one King in Heaven, the Lord Jesus Christ, King of kings, Lord of lords. The quicker we realize that it is neither about you nor me; it is always for the glory of Jesus and the building of the Kingdom of Heaven.

How can a Christian use the blood of Jesus as a weapon of warfare?

First: The previous Scripture passages were written for your encouragement and understanding about how the blood of Jesus is divinely powerful to accomplish His on-going purpose. As Andrae Crouch wrote, "The blood will never lose its power."

Second: In prayer, we who follow Jesus can apply His precious blood to our situation. We can humbly ask Jesus to engage into our need, bringing His blood with all its characteristics for victory. In our mind's eye, we can picture the blood being administered to bring healing, deliverance, order from confusion, or anointing over a new house/project/building.

Third: We can ask the Lord to cover us with His blood prior to entering ministry opportunities, to keep us safe from any enemy attacks. In a similar way, after street ministry, participants could pray the blood of Jesus to cleanse, since many demonic forces were encountered on the street.

Fourth: Praying the blood confronts any plans that the devil may have to bring confusion or destruction on the Church and the individuals that are seeking to follow Jesus, to being His witnesses to the world. The blood of Jesus renders the devil powerless, and keeps him in bondage. We should pray the blood of Jesus over our children, grandchildren and places of worship and learning, we can seal them for the glory of Jesus and deny darkness.

When we have been purchased by the blood of Jesus, it provides protection, forgiveness, life, redemption, fellowship with our Heavenly Father, sanctification, cleansing and victory over the devil. A good practical prayer at times would be something like this; would you like to pray this with me?

'Lord Jesus, I claim Your Blood to gain victory today for Your Glory. I bind you satan by the Blood of Jesus shed on the cross for my victory and affirm you are defeated. Amen'

Conditions for Pleading the Blood

Pleading the blood of Jesus over a person, or in a situation, is not some kind of magical solution, it is enforcing what has already been won at Calvary.

But there are conditions which need to be met for the Lord to make the blood available for our victory.

1.   A pure heart - this is covered in more detail in the chapter on obedience, nevertheless, it is obvious that if a person is living in rebellion against Jesus then it is quite ludicrous to expect Jesus to bless him. The fact He does at times, only proves His mercy. We may be experiencing problems because of our sin, rather than demonic attack.

2.   The Lord's Will must be fulfilled - a saintly person who has a terminal illness may have completed his work on Earth, and the Lord is ready to take him to a Heavenly reward. Regardless of how many people will pray, fast and plead the blood for healing; it is simply not the Will of Jesus.

3.   Pleading the blood – it does not work for selfish desires. To plead the blood for the correct card in a poker game, or for an athlete to make a successful play in a game, is not normally of much eternal value. I cannot stress enough that the blood of Jesus, nor any weapon of spiritual warfare, is not for selfish benefit.

As we use the blood of Jesus as a weapon in our warfare, we may not see any change immediately. Yet change will happen, as Scripture says, '*And they overcame him because of the blood of the Lamb, and because of the word of their testimony.*' Revelation 12:11

A King's Call to Prayer

Winston Churchill called it, "Our finest hour," but the situation at Dunkirk was bleak. In May 1940, Germany invaded Belgium, the Netherlands, Luxembourg and France. The Nazi Blitzkrieg swept into France at lightning speed surprising everyone in their path. The British Army was soon trapped, and there was a fear they would be destroyed.

At this crucial hour, on 23 May 1940, King George VI issued a call for a National Day of Prayer to be held on Sunday, 26 May. Almost immediately after the proclamation was given, everything changed. The British military leaders began their planning of the evacuation. The famous miracle at Dunkirk began.

The first miracle was the unexplained sudden halt of the German land forces on 24 May. The Nazis did not advance again until June. The Germans had every military advantage, such as superior troop strength, control of the skies with superior air power and their momentum. The British were confused, in retreat, and were trapped. In spite of these overwhelming advantages, the Germans stopped their pursuit of the British and to this day, there is much debate to explain the reason.

Although Goering's Luftwaffe continued to pound the British forces on the coast, the Army never attacked. The British assembled an armada to rescue the soldiers. Most reports stressed attention on the small crafts such as individual fishing boats which could only carry a few soldiers. The larger British vessels were the means for most soldiers to get away. Before the Germans renewed their attack, more than 300,000 British soldiers were returned safely to the British Isles, to fight another day.

While there are many explanations for this "miracle," the fact remains when King George issued his call for prayer, things started changing. In Daniel 6, Daniel was placed overnight in a lion's den. The Lord closed the mouths of the lions. In the same way, the Lord closed the mouth of the German army.

Heaven was listening when the prayers of the British people pleaded for the mercy and intervention of Jesus. The churches were reportedly filled on Sunday, all across the United Kingdom. There is a lie prevailing over the world today that the Lord does not answer prayer, and that prayer is a waste of time, "Whatever will be, will be." The events of May 1940 on the coast of France are proof that the Lord does get involved, especially when humbly invited into our situation. We need to be people of prayer, and in the process, change the world by seeing prayer answered. Like in that story of World War II, the Israelites experienced the same. They were on the run, but the Red Sea stood between them and a limited time when they would be captured or killed. God asks Moses, "*What is that in your hand?*" (Exodus 4:2) As Moses lifted up his rod, the Red Sea split and God's children escaped to fight another day. God is asking us, His Church today, 'What is that I have put within you?' Allow it to rise up, and see the Red Sea that surrounds us split!

CHAPTER 10

Intercessory Prayer

Successful spiritual warfare must include intercessory prayer, and successful intercession must include spiritual warfare. We invade the enemy's camp through intercessory prayers. Since spiritual warfare is a non-stop wrestling match, our intercessory prayer must be continuous. We must never cease in our intercession for others.

Prayer is a weapon of warfare.

'With all prayer and petition pray at all times in the Spirit, and with this in view, be on the alert with all perseverance and petition for all the saints, and pray on my behalf, that utterance may be given to me in the opening of my mouth, to make known with boldness the mystery of the gospel.' Ephesians 6:18

The apostle Paul, in his description of the full armor of God to conduct the spiritual warfare "against the spiritual forces of wickedness in the heavenly places", closes his thoughts with instruction to pray. Prayer is vital!

There are many types of prayer. There is petition, praise, repentance, warfare prayer, thanksgiving and intercession. For the purpose of strategic spiritual warfare, we will take a close look at the weapon of intercessory prayer.

Intercessory prayer is simple. It is praying for others. More specifically, it is standing before the Lord, pleading the case of another. We must be careful, however, because sometimes when we think we are praying for others, we are praying for ourselves.

Here is an example: "Lord make my boss a Christian!" Our true motive is, "I want my work to be easier!"

When I was having fellowship with a group from Iran, I felt as if I was living in the Book of Acts, having sweet fellowship with these amazing Christians. These people lived under daily persecution. As a new Christian, they would immediately lose their jobs, be imprisoned or be murdered, all under the watchful eye of a government. With all of this, they professed genuine love for the evil Moslem authorities, which is intercessory prayer in its purist form.

Intercessory prayer is standing in the gap for another, like Jesus did for us, seeking no payment back in return.

The Intercession Chapter

If I Corinthians 13 is the "love" chapter, and Hebrews 11 the "faith" chapter, it could be said, that Ezekiel 22 is the "intercession" chapter.

A detailed study of this chapter reveals the many sins observed by the Lord in Ezekiel's day. There was a conspiracy between priests, prophets, princes and the people, that has (v25) devoured lives, taken treasure and precious things; they have made many widows in the midst of her.

This chapter is filled with the wrath of the Lord, strongly proclaiming His displeasure with the actions and attitudes of His people. A study of this chapter will reveal a long list of sins which has angered the Lord. After a long discouraging description of the evils of the society and the corrupt leaders, the key verse is:

'I searched for a man among them who would build up the wall and stand in the gap before Me for the land, so that I would not destroy it; but I found no one. Thus I have poured out My indignation on them...' Ezekiel 22:30-31

Ezekiel has many military references, and can be understood as we picture a broken wall, with soldiers standing in the gap to protect the residents of the city.

In this we see that the Lord is fully prepared for two things.

First, in His righteous anger, He is ready to destroy the land.

Second, He is waiting to find someone who will stand before Him, to plead the case.

The Lord wants to see His people standing between Him and the sinners, generating intercession. For true spiritual warriors are those who rise to defend the innocent and attack evil. In other words, they stand in the gap.

The Lord is clearly angry at the sin of His people, but He appears angrier because there is nobody who will "stand in the gap" pleading for His mercy. This reminds me of the passage in 2 Peter when he gives a reason for Jesus' delay in returning to the earth.

'The Lord is not slow about His promise, as some count slowness, but is patient toward you, not wishing for any to perish but for all to come to repentance.' 2 Peter 3:9

It seems that the Lord is saying that it is up to the Christians to act in obedience to Christ, and influence the world for Jesus. Because we are not doing it, and because we are not winning the world for Jesus, He must be patient because of His love for the lost. It is His desire for them to know Him also, and be blessed. Could it be, that if we want Him to return sooner, we need to step up to the standard of Christ?

Two spiritual giants in the Lord are Paul and Moses. Scripture shows them standing in the gap, performing intercessory prayer.

In Romans 9:3, Paul states '*For I could wish that I myself were accursed, separated from Christ for the sake of my brethren, my kinsmen according to the flesh.*'

Moses, in Exodus 32:33, tells the Lord, if He cannot forgive the sin of Israel, then please "*blot me out from your book.*"

Both these giants of the faith showed their true love and devotion for others as they prayed, "Lord, send me to hell if it would provide forgiveness for Your people."

This is true standing in the gap, intercessory prayer. Most of our prayers today are simply saying, "Lord, remember and bless my pastor." "Remember and bless my neighbor." "Remember and bless the missionaries."

I see intensity in Paul and Moses, which is needed desperately today if we are to make a difference for the Kingdom of Heaven. This kind of intensity can only be described as warfare prayer.

The Lord is looking for someone to intercede by "standing in the gap" and asking/pleading for mercy. In fact, there is evidence that the anger and disappointment of the Lord is not so much in the sin of those who are disobedient, but in the lack of intercession on the part of His people.

Isaiah records that the Lord was astonished because there was no one to intercede.

'*Yes, truth is lacking; and he who turns aside from evil makes himself a prey. Now the Lord saw, and it was displeasing in His sight that there was no justice. And He saw that there was no man, and was astonished that there was no one to intercede; Then His own arm brought salvation to Him and His righteousness upheld Him.*' Isaiah 59:15-16

Jesus expects His people to be involved in intercessory prayer.

Paul writes in 1 Thessalonians 5:17 that we are to pray without ceasing. While this means for us to always be in an attitude of prayer, there are people who have told me they run out of things to ask God for. Those involved with intercessory prayer will never run out of people and situations.

Stephen was the first Christian martyr. As he was being stoned, he cried out with a loud voice, (Acts 7:60) *"Lord, do not hold this sin against them!"* With Stephen's last breath he was fulfilling Ezekiel 22 and standing in the gap, praying for those who had just killed him. Intercessory prayer is simple but not always easy.

Intercessory prayer is a powerful weapon to break the hold of demonic forces over people, places and events in our world. The devil will not merely stand by and watch the Church get involved in effective intercessory prayer. There are many ways the devil will keep us off our knees, to prevent intercessory prayer.

For example: Have you ever decided to take prayer more seriously and almost immediately there are distractions placed in your way? A thought of something you forgot to do, a person you have been intending to call, a bill which needs to be paid, or even a question about some Bible verse which you feel compelled to re-read. Other distractions could be a phone call, a knock on the door, a sudden twinge of pain somewhere in your body or a hundred of other things which causes our attention to be diverted from praying for those in need.

We need to resist the devil, and make new commitments to get involved in intercessory prayer, to change the world.

It seems that leaders have a special duty to provide intercession for their people. In 1 Samuel 12:23, Samuel tells the people of Israel, *'Moreover, as for me, far be it from me that I should sin against the Lord by ceasing to pray for you...'*

This is a strong admonition for pastors and anyone else who deems or sees themselves as leaders in a church. If there is a common theme of the conversations at denominational gatherings, it is the pastors telling the horror stories about the problems with their congregations. There is almost constant war between the people and the pastors in many congregations. No wonder they are not shining for the Kingdom of God.

The writer to the Hebrews even describes Jesus as the Great High Priest (or in today's society a pastor) who lives to make intercession for them. (Hebrews 7:24-25). Jesus is our best role model. There is a picture presented similar to a courtroom.

There is our Heavenly Father as judge. The devil is the prosecuting attorney who is bringing charges against the Christian. And the devil is really pouring it on. He brings indisputable evidence complete with testimonies from others, video tapes of the Christian's sins and a knowledge of the Scriptures to prove the believer guilty. He presents an open and shut case. The third major figure in this Heavenly courtroom is Jesus Himself. He is making intercession. "Father; this sin has already been paid by My death on the cross. This Christian has placed his trust in Me and has received a Royal pardon."

Our Heavenly Father proclaims, "Not guilty by the blood of the Lamb!" Next case!

This intercessory prayer by pastors for all members of their church family is critical, especially in the light of Scripture. Pastors, take up your responsibility and stand in the gap for your people!

'From everyone who has been given much, much will be required; and to whom they entrusted much, of him they will ask all the more.' Luke 12:48

The Church today would be so much stronger if there was more intercessory prayer for the lay leaders on the part of the pastors. In fact, James warns teachers (which are the pastors today) will incur a stricter judgment.

'Let not many of you become teachers, my brethren, knowing that as such we will incur a stricter judgment.' James 3:1

One reason many congregations face division and struggle is because pastors fail to spend time in God. What do I mean by that? They have a quick prayer in the morning out of habit or duty, then off into appointments for the rest of the day and night. Christianity is not about appointments but relationship. And it is in that relationship with God that Pastors will hear the voice of God, sense the need of his flock from the prayer closet, to be in the right place at the right time with the right people, sharing the right word. It is time for us all, especially pastors, to step up and make that which is wrong in our relationship with God, right. Time to realize, that the importance of our week is not standing in front of our flock, but kneeling at His feet knowing that without Him we are nothing. From this position, we can confront the gates of hell with intercessory prayer, we will see mighty breakthroughs as those gates come crashing down.

As Jeremiah 29:7 states

'Seek the welfare of the city where I have sent you into exile, and pray to the Lord on its behalf; for in its welfare you will have welfare.'

In Matthew 24, it tells about the second coming of Jesus Christ, an event which has given us great hope, but also great division in the body of Christ because of the question - when will Jesus return?

Matthew 24:14 tells us. *'This Gospel of the Kingdom shall be preached in the whole world to all the nations and then the end shall come.'*

We should pray for the return of Jesus to the Earth, to end this era and usher in the Kingdom of God. But we should pray intelligently. We should not pray, "Jesus come back." We should pray for the evangelization of the world. We should pray specifically for missionaries and Christians in parts of the world where the name of Jesus is not heard. There are many people, groups who have never heard the name "Jesus." There is much work to be done for everyone in the world to learn about Jesus.

Here's a simple exercise! Find a world map on your computer, smart-phone or book. Lay hands on the map then pray for the people in those countries. Sense in your heart a country and then specifically pray for it, and continue to pray for it until you sense the country burden lifts off your heart. Perhaps learn about a nation or area, so that intelligent prayers can be made on their behalf. We can pray for the Christians who are there. We can pray for hearts to be receptive when the Gospel is presented. We can pray for the Christians who will be going there, perhaps many years from now in some cases. As we open our hearts and minds to hear from the Lord, He will eagerly share His heart for those nations, and will allow us to partner with Him as they are won for the Kingdom of Heaven.

It is all evangelism, from the evangelist preaching on the street to those who are praying for him in any place around the world. The evangelist needs the prayer of his supporters to be successful. In fact, a type of intercessory prayer is through prayer partners.

A good practice is for each Christian to have one or more prayer partner. Each partner will pray in faith that the Lord will provide for the need of his partner. Each partner is interceding for his partner. When you have more than one prayer partner, learn to know what they hold the keys to, more than the other prayer partner, as also yourself. Each one of us can have a gifting on an area and therefore can see further than another. Use those who God has placed around you to further the Gospel, by allowing their gifting to come into effect in your life.

Another guide to successful intercessory prayer is to pray from Heaven's point of view.

'*Set your mind of the things above, not on the things that are on earth.*' Colossians 3:2

'*(God) raised us up with Him, and seated us with Him in the heavenly places in Christ Jesus.*' Ephesians 2:6

Never be fearful to ask the Lord for direction when involved with intercessory prayer. During our Silk Road prayer outreach in 2010, our group was in Peking, China. The Lord asked us to pray for the church in Peking. So we interceded by asking the Lord to protect the Christians. We stood in the gap, beseeching the Lord to provide for their needs, to give them boldness, to protect them, to teach them, and to use the church in Peking as a light to those still walking in darkness.

As our outreach continued into Western China, the direction from the Lord changed. We were in an area where there were very few Christians. In spite of the fact that we had contact with a couple of Christian cell groups, and we did pray with them and for them, the Lord led us to be in prayer for the people who were lost. Specifically, we prayed for hearts to be softened so that they can receive the Word when it arrives. The parable of the sower (Matthew 13:1-23) tells us of various types of soil. There was hard soil, shallow soil, soil with many weeds and good soil. The Word which came to those four soils had different results. So, we felt the Lord wanted us to pray, when the Word of the Lord came into Western China with power, the hearts of the people would receive it with joy and expectancy.

It was a wonderful experience to climb to a high hillside overlooking a city in order to pray for the city. We were proclaiming the Word to combat the demons who had been in control for many centuries. We had a word from the Lord that the Gospel of Jesus Christ was en route, and we were like an advance party to prepare the way.

Prayer is work and a big part of prayer work is to develop a relationship with Jesus, providing clear communication from Him on who to pray for, and how to pray for them.

Sometimes it is necessary to intercede without knowing who is guilty, as in the case explained in Deuteronomy 21.

(v1) – 'If a slain person is found ... it is not known who has struck *him. (v3) ... the city which is nearest to the slain man ... the elders of that city, shall take a heifer ... (4) and shall break the heifer's neck ... (v7) 'Our hands did not shed this bleed, nor did our eyes see it. (v8) Forgive Your people Israel whom You have redeemed, O Lord, and do not place the guilt of innocent blood in the midst of Your people Israel.' And the bloodguiltiness shall be forgiven them.'*

Intercession and the Return of Jesus

A topic of interest for many Christians is what can be called the Second Coming of Jesus Christ. Books such as Hal Lindsey's, *Late, Great Planet Earth* and the *Left Behind* series by Tim LaHaye & Jerry Jenkins are extremely popular. Many, if not most Christians, believe that the return of Jesus, and the end of the world as we know it, is imminent. I would respectfully like to offer my opinion that the return of Jesus will not occur until three conditions are met.

1. The Evangelization of the World - Matthew 24:14 *'This gospel of the kingdom shall be preached in the whole world as a testimony to all the nations, and then the end will come.'*

2. The Nation of Israel will acknowledge Jesus Christ as the Messiah.

3. There will be a Unity in the body of Christ. (See my Unity chapter)

These three conditions would appear to be the perfect topics for intense intercessory prayer. We need more prayer for the evangelization of the World, for Israel and the Jews, and Christian Unity.

Your prayer can change things!

The Bible says, *'the effective prayer of a righteous man can accomplish much.'* James 5:16

Do you really believe that your prayers can accomplish much? The Church should be bursting with righteous people empowered with the Holy Spirit, praying in the Spirit for the Kingdom to come on earth as it is in Heaven. In fact righteousness as demonstrated through obedience is another powerful weapon in our strategic spiritual warfare.

No person can be righteous in his own merit. Our righteousness comes totally from the Righteousness of Jesus Christ.

One last major point as we examine intercessory prayer is a look at some principles for effective intercessory prayer, compiled by Joy Dawson. This is a detailed "recipe" for effective intercessory prayer.

1. Praise The Lord for the privilege of engaging in the same wonderful ministry as the Lord Jesus (Hebrews 7:25). Praise Jesus for the privilege of cooperating with Him in the affairs of men.

2. Make sure your heart is clean before Jesus, by having given the Holy Spirit time to convict, should there be any unconfessed sin (Psalm 66:18; Psalm 139:23-24). Check carefully to make sure that you do not harbor unforgiveness or resentment toward anyone (Matthew 6:12; Mark 11:25). Job had to forgive his friends for their wrong judgment of him, before he could pray effectively for them (Job 42:10).

3. Acknowledge you cannot really pray without the direction and energy of the Holy Spirit (Romans 8:26). Ask Him to utterly control you by His Spirit, receive by faith He will, and thank Him (Hebrews 11:6).

4. Die to your own imaginations, desires and burdens for what you feel you should pray (Proverbs 3:5, 6; 28:26; Isaiah 55:8).

5. Deal aggressively with the enemy. Come against him in the all-powerful Name of the Lord Jesus Christ and with the "sword of the Spirit", the Word of God (James 4:7).

6. Praise Jesus now in faith for the remarkable prayer meeting

that you are going to have. He is a remarkable God and will do something consistent with His character.

7. Wait before Jesus in silent expectancy, listening for His direction (Psalm 62:5; Micah 7:7; Psalm 81:11-13).

8. In obedience and faith, utter what The Lord brings to your mind, believing (John 10:27). Keep asking The Holy Spirit for direction in relation to whom or what you are praying for, expecting Him to answer. He promises to guide and direct you (Psalm 32:8). Make sure that you do not move on to the next subject until you've given Jesus time to discharge all He wants to say to you regarding this particular burden; especially when praying in a group. Be encouraged from the lives of Moses, Daniel, Paul and Anna. The Lord gives revelation to those who make intercession a way of life.

9. If possible have your Bible with you, should Jesus give you direction or confirmation from it (Psalm 119:105).

10. When The Lord ceases to bring things to your mind in prayer, finish by praising, and thanking Him for what He has done, reminding yourself of Romans 11:36.

In plain language, intercessory prayer is praying for others. However, a closer examination of the whole range of intercessory prayer creates a vast realm of intervening for the spiritual well-being of others. Intercessory prayer can be the adventure of a lifetime. It attacks the very gates of hell for the glory of Jesus Christ. What a wonderful opportunity to be blessed and be a blessing to millions of people who we will meet in Heaven one day.

CHAPTER 11

Bible Intercessors

The Bible is filled with examples of intercessory prayer. Intercessory prayer comes from all sorts of people, situations and needs. While I cannot list every example of intercessory prayer in the Bible; I would like to focus on a few. The Bible tells us of several intercessor warriors, whom we can study and gain better understanding.

Jesus

In John 17, Jesus prays what some scholars have called, "The High Priestly Prayer."

'I ask on their behalf; I do not ask on behalf of the world, but of those whom You have given Me; for they are Yours; and all things that are Mine are Yours, and Yours are Mine; and I have been glorified in them. I am no longer in the world; and yet they themselves are in the world, and I come to You. Holy Father, keep them in Your name, the name which You have given Me, that they may be one even as We are. While I was with them, I was keeping them in Your name which You have given Me; and I guarded them and not one of them perished but the son of perdition, so that the Scripture would be

fulfilled. But now I come to You; and these things I speak in the world so that they may have My joy made full in themselves. I have given them Your word; and the world has hated them, because they are not of the world, even as I am not of the world. I do not ask You to take them out of the world, but to keep them from the evil one. They are not of the world, even as I am not of the world. Sanctify them in the truth; Your word is truth. As You sent Me into the world, I also have sent them into the world. For their sakes I sanctify Myself, that they themselves also may be sanctified in truth. "I do not ask on behalf of these alone, but for those also who believe in Me through their word; that they may all be one; even as You, Father, are in Me and I in You, that they also may be in Us, so that the world may believe that You sent Me.' John 17:9-21

Abraham

Genesis 18:17-33 tells us of the conversation between Abraham and the Lord on behalf of the people of Sodom. At first Abraham asks if fifty righteous people could be found, would the city be afforded destruction. The Lord agreed. Of course, Abraham must have visited the city since his nephew lived there and he knew it was not likely that there were fifty righteous. So he pressed in a bit asking that if the fifty were lacking only five, could the city be spared? The Lord responded by saying if forty-five were found, the city would not be destroyed. To make a long story short, Abraham bartered his way down to ten righteous, and the Lord agreed if ten were found He would relent.

While ten were not found and the city was left in fire and brimstone, the main point of the passage was the Lord's pleasure with Abraham for his heart of intercession for people he certainly did not appreciate nor understand. Yet as a man of faith, he stood in the gap between the Lord and the people of Sodom.

Moses

Moses seemed to be in continual intercessory prayer for his people. Below are two examples.

In Numbers the Lord informs Moses,

'*I will smite them with pestilence and dispossess them, and I will make you into a nation greater and mightier than they.*' Numbers 14:12

Can you imagine this opportunity Moses was given? He could have been rid of these people who were driving him crazy. They were constantly bickering and complaining about everything under the sun. He was now given an opportunity to be "let off the hook." How many pastors would revel in such a word from the Lord? But Moses had a love for his people. He immediately launched into intercession pleading with the Lord to forgive. He reminded the Lord of His nature and character. (v18) The Lord is slow to anger and abundant in loving kindness. And the Lord responded in v20, "*I have pardoned them according to your word.*"

After the Lord sent fiery serpents among the people for complaining, '*So the people came to Moses and said, 'We have sinned, because we have spoken against the Lord and you; intercede with the Lord, that He may remove the serpents from us.' And Moses interceded for the people.*' Numbers 21:7

This is also an example of intercession requiring more than saying a simple prayer. Moses was instructed to make a bronze serpent and hang it on a standard. If anyone bitten by a serpent would look to the bronze serpent, he would live. Jesus used this as a simile, making a comparison. As the people who were dying, looked up to the bronze serpent and lived; those lost in sin and dying could look to Jesus for salvation.

Elders instructed to intercede

'If a slain person is found lying in the open country in the land which the Lord your God gives you to possess, and it is not known who has struck him, then your elders and your judges shall go out and measure the distance to the cities which are around the slain one... all the elders of that city which is nearest to the slain man shall wash their hands over the heifer whose neck was broken in the valley, and they shall answer and say, 'Our hands did not shed this blood, nor did our eyes see it. Forgive Your people Israel whom You have redeemed, O Lord, and do not place the guilt of innocent blood in the midst of Your people Israel.' And the blood guiltiness shall be forgiven them.' Deuteronomy 21:1-8

Samuel

Samuel makes a promise to the people of Israel after he is rejected and they demand a King.

'Moreover, as for me, far be it from me that I should sin against the Lord by ceasing to pray for you; but I will instruct you in the good and right way.'

I Samuel 12:23

Abigail

In I Samuel 25, Nabal insulted King David's men. David took 200 soldiers and intended to kill Nabal but Abigail, Nabal's wife, interceded on Nabal's behalf.

'Then Abigail hurried and took two hundred loaves of bread and two jugs of wine and five sheep already prepared and five measures of roasted grain and a hundred clusters of raisins and two hundred cakes of figs, and loaded them on donkeys. She said to her young men, 'Go on before me; behold, I am coming after you." But she did

not tell her husband Nabal. It came about as she was riding on her donkey and coming down by the hidden part of the mountain, that behold, David and his men were coming down toward her; so she met them. Now David had said, 'Surely in vain I have guarded all that this man has in the wilderness, so that nothing was missed of all that belonged to him; and he has returned me evil for good. May God do so to the enemies of David, and more also, if by morning I leave as much as one male of any who belong to him.' When Abigail saw David, she hurried and dismounted from her donkey, and fell on her face before David and bowed herself to the ground. She fell at his feet and said, 'On me alone, my lord, be the blame. And please let your maidservant speak to you, and listen to the words of your maidservant. Please do not let my lord pay attention to this worthless man, Nabal, for as his name is, so is he. Nabal is his name and folly is with him; but I your maidservant did not see the young men of my lord whom you sent. Now therefore, my lord, as the LORD lives, and as your soul lives, since the LORD has restrained you from shedding blood, and from avenging yourself by your own hand, now then let your enemies and those who seek evil against my lord, be as Nabal. Now let this gift which your maidservant has brought to my lord be given to the young men who accompany my lord. Please forgive the transgression of your maidservant; for the LORD will certainly make for my lord an enduring house, because my lord is fighting the battles of the LORD, and evil will not be found in you all your days. Should anyone rise up to pursue you and to seek your life, then the life of my lord shall be bound in the bundle of the living with the LORD your God; but the lives of your enemies He will sling out as from the hollow of a sling. And when the LORD does for my lord according to all the good that He has spoken concerning you, and appoints you ruler over Israel this will not cause grief or a troubled heart to my lord, both by having shed blood without cause and by my lord having avenged himself. When the LORD deals well with my lord, then remember your maidservant.' Then David said to Abigail, 'Blessed be the LORD God of Israel, who sent you this day to meet me, and blessed be your discernment, and blessed be you, who have kept me this day from bloodshed and from avenging myself by my own hand. Nevertheless, as the LORD God of Israel lives, who has restrained me from harming you, unless you had come quickly to meet me, surely there would not have been left to Nabal until the morning light as much as one male.' So David received from her hand what she had brought him and said to her, 'Go up to your house in peace. See, I have listened to you and granted your request.' 1 Samuel 25:18-35

Abigail later became the wife of David after Nabal's death. It is obvious David was impressed with her and took her as his bride.

Hezekiah

As Hezekiah was a Godly King in Judah, he sought for all Jews to celebrate the Passover and he sent messengers throughout all of Judah and Israel, inviting everyone to Jerusalem. Now the nation of Israel was not a part of Judah or Jerusalem, and had their own places of worship. While most people laughed and mocked the messengers, there were some who agreed to participate in the Passover. This was unusual and they had no experience with the Passover or the proper way to conduct themselves.

The Jewish law is very strict about the observance of the Passover and many were unclean. Therefore, Hezekiah interceded.

'For a multitude of the people, even many from Ephraim and Manasseh, Issachar, and Zebulon had not purified themselves, yet they ate the Passover otherwise than prescribed. For Hezekiah prayed for them, saying, 'May the good Lord pardon everyone who prepares his heart to seek God, the Lord God of his fathers, though not according to the purification rules of the sanctuary.' So the Lord heard Hezekiah and healed the people.' 2 Chronicles 30:18-20

Elijah

Elijah was told it was going to rain after a long drought. He began to intercede for rain. The Bible is full of promises telling us what Jesus will do. This provides us a wonderful opportunity to partner with Him by praying for the promise to be fulfilled.

'Elijah went up to the top of Carmel; and he couched down on the earth and put his face between his knees. He said to his servant, 'Go up now, look toward the sea.' So he went up and looked and said, 'There is nothing.' And he said, 'Go back' seven times. It came about at the seventh time, that he said, 'Behold, a cloud as small as a man's hand is coming up from the sea.' And he said, 'Go up, say to Ahab, Prepare your chariot and go down, so that the heavy shower does not stop you.' In a little while the sky grew black with clouds and wind, and there was a heavy shower.' 1 Kings 18:42-45

Esther

The book of Esther is unique because it is the only book in the Bible which does not contain the word "God." The book is primarily the story of how God's chosen people, the Jews, were saved from annihilation while in the Persian Empire. Esther is a Jewish woman who becomes the queen of Persia. But because of some tricks on the part of Haman, the king issues a decree for every Jew is to be killed. The king does not know his new queen is Jewish, and Esther believes she must do something to rescue her people. There is intercessory prayer and fasting for Esther as she prepares to speak to the king. Esther goes to the king and intercedes for her people, symbolizing that we can go to the King of Kings (Jesus) to intercede for our people today.

Notice the fear which prevailed prior to Esther entering the presence of the king, who was after all her husband. But when the king saw Esther, he was pleased to welcome her and proclaimed he would give her anything she requested up to half of his kingdom. Many Christians have a mental picture of a God who is very harsh. Some remember only the verses about His wrath. As a result, many have a total misunderstanding about the Fear of the Lord. Jesus eagerly wants us to approach Him. We are to come boldly to the throne of Grace. Just as Esther was the bride of the king. We, the Church, are the bride of Christ and we can enter into His presence with joy and confidence. As the bride of Ahasuerus did, when she went to her king to intercede for her people, just as the Church needs to do. The Western Church should intercede for the persecuted Church struggling to be light and life in the midst of harassment, arrests and death threats. The danger faced in our day is real, and deadly in many places around the world. The intercessory prayers for our brothers and sisters are vitally needed, and this involves warfare prayer.

Job

Job gives us a grand example of praying for children and family. Weekly he would sacrifice burnt offerings, and intercede on the possibility that one of his children sinned before the Lord.

'When the days of feasting had completed their cycle (each of Job's sons would host a feast), Job would send and consecrate them, rising up early in the morning and offering burnt offerings according to the number of them all; for Job said, 'Perhaps my sons have sinned and cursed God in their hearts.' Thus Job did continually.' Job 1:5

I know of parents who intercede for their children and grandchildren in rather unusual ways. For example, a couple started praying for the husband of their daughter, the day she was born. Too many parents do not approve of the boy their daughter is dating and they "panic pray", asking the Lord to take him out of her life. My friends are not in this position because they have prayed with confidence for their daughter's husband and have been doing so for years. They know the Lord will honor their prayers and they do not panic.

There are grandparents who have been praying for their grandchildren on a daily basis even before their children were even married. They believe the Lord stores up prayers in Heaven (Revelation 5:8) and will answer them in due time. They also want the best for their family, even if they should die before their grandchildren are born.

'The Lord restored the fortunes of Job when he prayed for his friends.' Job 42:10

Even after all the long discussion Job had with his comforters, he took time to provide intercessory prayer for them, after his ordeal was over.

Daniel

When Daniel faced a crisis because Nebuchadnezzar demanded a description and an interpretation to his dream, or he would have all the wise men killed; Daniel went to Shadrach, Meshach and Abednego to intercede for Daniel, while he sought the Lord's guidance.

'Then Daniel went to his house and informed his friends, Hananiah, Mishael and Azariah, about the matter, so that they might request compassion from the God of heaven concerning this mystery, so that Daniel and his friends would not be destroyed with the rest of the wise men of Babylon.' Daniel 2:17-18

Daniel 9 tells us that he discovered the Lord's decree that Israel was to spend 70 years in exile and the 70 years was nearing, he began to pray. He did not sit back and think that the Lord would automatically fulfill his word. Daniel was a man of intercession...

'So now, our God, listen to the prayer of Your servant and to his supplications, and for Your sake, O Lord, let Your face shine on Your desolate sanctuary. O my God, incline Your ear and hear! Open Your eyes and see our desolations and the city which is called by Your name; for we are not presenting our supplications before You on account of any merits of our own, but on account of Your great compassion O Lord, hear! O Lord, forgive! O Lord, listen and take action! For Your own sake, O my God, do not delay, because Your city and Your people are called by Your name.' Daniel 9:17-19

Paul

The apostle Paul writes to Timothy to intercede for governments when they were arresting, torturing, and putting Christians to death.

'First of all, then, I urge that entreaties and prayers, petitions and thanksgivings, be made on behalf of all men, for kings and all who are in authority, so that we may lead a tranquil and quiet life in all godliness and dignity.' 1 Timothy 2:1-2

Judah

There is a long drama when Joseph is sold into slavery by his brothers. Joseph is taken to Egypt, where he excels and eventually becomes the second most powerful man in the kingdom. There is a worldwide famine and his brothers come to Egypt to buy food. Joseph seems to be playing a cruel game and threatens to bind Benjamin into slavery, which would have broken the heart of Jacob, but Judah intercedes for Jacob before Joseph.

'Then Judah approached him, and said, 'Oh my lord, may your servant please speak a word in my lord's ears, and do not be angry with your servant; for you are equal to Pharaoh. My lord asked his servants, saying, 'Have you a father or a brother?' We said to my lord, 'We have an old father and a little child of his old age. Now his brother is dead, so he alone is left of his mother, and his father loves him.' Then you said to your servants, 'Bring him down to me that I may set my eyes on him.' But we said to my lord, 'The lad cannot leave his father, for if he should leave his father, his father would die.' You said to your servants, however, 'Unless your youngest brother comes down with you, you will not see my face again.' Thus it came about when we went up to your servant my father, we told him the words of my lord. Our father said, 'Go back, buy us a little food.' But we said, 'We cannot go down. If our youngest brother is with us, then

we will go down; for we cannot see the man's face unless our youngest brother is with us.' Your servant my father said to us, 'You know that my wife bore me two sons; and the one went out from me, and I said, 'Surely he is torn in pieces,' and I have not seen him since. If you take this one also from me, and harm befalls him, you will bring my gray hair down to Sheol in sorrow.' Now, therefore, when I come to your servant my father, and the lad is not with us, since his life is bound up in the lad's life, when he sees that the lad is not with us, he will die. Thus your servants will bring the gray hair of your servant our father down to Sheol in sorrow. For your servant became surety for the lad to my father, saying, 'If I do not bring him back to you, then let me bear the blame before my father forever.' Now, therefore, please let your servant remain instead of the lad a slave to my lord, and let the lad go up with his brothers. For how shall I go up to my father if the lad is not with me—for fear that I see the evil that would overtake my father?' Genesis 44:18-34

Immediately Joseph ordered all his staff to depart and he revealed himself to his brothers.

These are only a few examples of intercessory prayer in the Bible, but instead of reading about those names, imagine that it was your name you were reading about. Now ask yourself, "What is stopping you from interceding?" "Is Jesus a respecter of persons?" The answer is no! Therefore, arise and be the one who stands in the gap for the Master!

CHAPTER 12

Worship

Many think worship is just about singing, but in truth, worship is warfare. When we worship in Spirit and Truth, Jesus becomes our worship. When Jesus is worshiped, powerful forces are released from Heaven to move in us and around us to fulfill His purpose. Those same forces of light are in lethal combat against the forces of evil, which surround us, and seek to inhabit the world.

As we sing about the Cross, His Name, His blood, and surrender our will to His will; not only will our lives be changed for the better, but the world will be changed.

I hear you ask, "I don't see any changes!" Where "the will" of the worshiper is intact to self, then that is not true worship. That is adoration of self. True worship is when all hell is broke loose against you, and you don't want to worship. That small voice rises from the cries of the heart – then is where 'not I who lives but Christ who lives in me!' From that place draws the presence of God into your life, and those around you. Otherwise we have only empty praises, and worship in look that has no power.

The book of Revelation is about Praise and Worship, more than last day's prophecy. Revelation shows us the ultimate defeat of the demonic kingdom, and it is accomplished by constant worship of the Lamb who was slain.

The best example of worship in Scripture, is Revelation chapters 4 and 5. This passage allows us to witness worship in Heaven. As you read it, examine, and meditate on these two chapters. It is so easy to feel the power of worship constantly overcoming all darkness.

This worship is focused on Jesus. There are descriptions of thrones, twenty-four elders, a sea of glass like crystal, four living creatures and angels. However, the focus is the Lord. The twenty-four elders cast their crowns before the Lord and declare,

'Worthy are You, our Lord and our God, to receive glory and honor and power; for You created all things, and because of Your will they existed, and were created.' Revelation 4:11

The four living creatures do not cease to say,

'Holy, Holy, Holy is the Lord God, the Almighty, who was and who is and who is to come.' Revelation 4:8

Angels are saying with a loud voice,

'Worthy is the Lamb that was slain to receive power and riches and wisdom and might and honor and glory and blessing.' Revelation 5:12

Did you know worship in Heaven is noisy? Thirteen times the term, "a loud voice", is used in the Book of Revelation. Loud worship in Heaven is not easy for me to admit because I enjoy the softer moments. The older I get the more "easy listening" is my music of choice. Many Christians refer to a daily "quiet time" with the Lord. Nevertheless, Heaven is a place of noisy and exuberant worship. As we enter into this kind of worship, there is power over all the forces of darkness. As a congregation or individual spends quality time in worship, the Lord inhabits the praises of His people. As the power of the Lord is present in a building, or on a street, or in a neighborhood, in a city, or in a nation; then the powers of darkness will retreat. The long term or strategic benefits of worship will result in victory for the Kingdom of Heaven.

This victory may not be seen immediately. It may take years or even decades, but as we continue this kind of worship, we will see the results that will truly glorify Jesus Christ.

How can worship be used effectively in spiritual warfare?

1. Focus on Jesus, and not on the gifts nor miracles, nor healings, nor fancy preaching and/or music which is designed to entertain, not tradition, and not on trivial things like where the flowers are placed, or if the Communion cloths should be plain or fancy. The focus cannot be on us or things. We must focus on Jesus.

2. Sing Scripture and hymns based on the truth of the Bible. Especially sing hymns which focus on the weapons of our warfare. (More on this idea below)

3. Preach the Word, and read the Word, rather than a lot of man made poems written by the lost, and not consistent with Scripture.

There have been times when I have attended churches and I was greatly troubled. Most services lacked a sermon, or any proclamation of Biblical truth. The song service was very emotional and exciting, becoming very energetic and joyful. As the people continued in their singing, the service seemed to get carried away with the fun of the dancing. The pastor continued to encourage the songs and group singing. There was a definite "party" atmosphere. Then as the service progressed, an announcement was made: "There would be no sermon! The worship would continue." This decision on the part of the pastor was unfortunate because the singing portion had opened our hearts to receive the Word in power. The worship service changed from an opportunity for life changing preaching, into mere entertainment.

I wanted to scream, "Preaching is worship also." The apostle Paul writes in 1 Corinthians 14:26

'...When you assemble, each one has a psalm, has a teaching, has a revelation, has a tongue, and has an interpretation. Let all things be done for edification.'

What if someone had started reading Scripture, and then others started reading other Scriptures, until the time for the service had expired and there was no singing or preaching? Would it be welcomed with equal excitement by those who enjoy singing?

Worship is not designed to make us feel good: it is to honor Jesus and result in effective personal discipleship for the glory of the Kingdom of Heaven.

It was prayer and worship which brought down the walls of Jericho. The Israelites marched around Jericho for seven days. They did not do anything or say anything. They merely marched in obedience to the command of the Lord. This was strategic. I am certain every inhabitant of Jericho was feeling more than a little uneasy. They had heard about the mighty Army of the Lord. They had now seen them circling their city. Their hearts were fearful and uncertain. Then after all this marching, the people of Israel shouted Praise and the walls fell.

Nehemiah 9:3 tells us that Israel separated themselves from all foreigners and, '...read from the book of the law of the Lord their God for a fourth of the day; and for another fourth they confessed and worshiped the Lord their God.'

These actions were a combination of the Word, confession, repentance and worship. This also occurred during a time of group fasting. They used four strategic weapons in their successful battle to rebuild Jerusalem. As the Church today enters into pure worship, and embraces other weapons of strategic spiritual warfare, we will see the Kingdom of Heaven become the reality we want and need

Here are some hymns relating to spiritual warfare weapons...

The Cross

"Power of the Cross" written by Keith and Kristen Getty
"Wonder of the Cross" by Robin Mark

"At the Cross" by Isaac Watts
"Near the Cross" by Fanny Crosby
"The Old Rugged Cross" by George Bennard
"When I Survey the Wondrous Cross" by Isaac Watts
"At Calvary" by William Newell
"Beneath the Cross of Jesus" by Elizabeth Clephane

The Name of Jesus

"In the Name of Jesus" (unknown author)
"At the Name of Jesus" by Caroline Noel
"All Hail the Power of Jesus Name" by Edward Perronet
"Blessed Be the Name" by Matt Redmon
"There is Something about that Name" by Bill & Gloria Gaither
"Jesus, Name above all Names" by Bill Batstone
"How Sweet the Name of Jesus Sounds" by John Newton
"Lord, I Lift Your Name on High" by Rick Founds

The Blood of Jesus

"Power in the Blood" by Lewis Jones
"Washed in the Blood" by Elisha Hoffman
"Nothing but the Blood" by Robert Lowry
"My Hope is Built on Nothing Less than Jesus Blood and Righteousness" by Edward Mote

Christian Unity

"Bind us Together" by Bob Gillman
"We Being Many, Are One Body" by Marty Goetz
"They Will Know We Are Christians by Our Love" by Peter Scholtes
"The Church's One Foundation" by Samuel Stone

Obedience
"Trust and Obey" by John Sammis
"Have Thine Own Way, Lord!" By Adelaide Pollard

Prayer

"Sweet Hour of Prayer" by Rev W W Walford
"What a Friend We Have in Jesus" by Joseph Scriven
"Make My Life a Prayer to You" by Keith Green

The Word (Bible)

"The B.I.B.L.E, That's the Book for Me"
"How Firm a Foundation" by John Rippon
"Standing on the Promises of God" by R. Kelso Carter
"Ancient Words" by Michael W. Smith
"Wonderful Words of Life" by Philip Paul Bliss
"Thy Word" by Amy Grant
"Break Thou the Bread of Life" by Mary Lathbury, Alexander Groves, and William Sherwin

Humility

"Amazing Grace" by John Newton
"Just as I Am" by Charlotte Elliott and William Bradbury

As the Church experiences worship in Spirit and in Truth, the Holy Spirit will inhabit the praises of His people, and will accomplish His purposes in their lives. This inhabitation of the Holy Spirit will protect, cleanse, encourage, and prepare for victorious service for the Kingdom of Heaven. Let us therefore worship often and sincerely for the glory of Jesus Christ.

CHAPTER 13

Humility

Paul urges Christians to have the same attitude as Jesus.

'Do nothing from selfishness or empty conceit, but with humility of mind let each of you regard one another as more important than himself; do not merely look out for your own personal interests, but also for the interests of others. Have this attitude in yourselves which was also in Christ Jesus, who although He existed in the form of God, did not regard equality with God a thing to be grasped, but emptied Himself, taking the form of a bondservant, and being made in the likeness of men. And being found in appearance as a man, He humbled Himself by becoming obedient to the point of death, even death on a cross.' Philippians 2:3-8

This is a powerful and well written account of what Jesus did. It deserves to be studied carefully and thoroughly.

If Jesus had left the splendor of Heaven and came to Earth as a wealthy man, with the best house to live in, the best food to eat, the finest of clothes to wear, the finest healthcare and the most luxurious forms of transportation available; it would have been a tremendous act of humility. The best of Earth is worse than slums of Heaven (not that Heaven has slums, but you should know what I mean).

But Jesus went further. He emptied Himself, taking on the form of a bondservant. Servant and slave have the same meaning in the Greek. Jesus became a slave. He said in Matthew 20:28, *"just as the Son of Man did not come to be served, but to serve, and to give His life a ransom for many."*

Think of the difference between the world's wealthiest man living in total splendor and the homeless beggar. Jesus became like the homeless beggar. He had nothing. He had to borrow a coin to give an object lesson on giving to Caesar what is Caesars' and to God what is God's, as written in Matthew 22:17-21.

Jesus went further than taking on the form of a slave. If He had lived out His life as a slave, constantly serving and doing for others, it would have been a great example of humility.

However, Jesus also came to die, not only to live with few earthly comforts, but to actually lay down His life was a great act of emptying. If He had faced a firing squad or a modern day lethal injection; it would have been a noble demonstration of His service.

But Jesus did not just die; He faced death on the Cross. He willingly faced the torture, shame, and brutality of the worst possible way to die devised by man. This was the act of humility as Paul described in his letter to the Philippians.

What was the result of this act of humility? '*At the Name of Jesus, every knee will bow and every tongue will confess that Jesus is Lord to the Glory of the Father.*' Philippians 2:10

The humility of Jesus is found not only in Philippians 2, but many times in the gospel writings. An examination of Jesus' ministry shows humility in action.

'*But the man who was healed did not know who it was, for Jesus had slipped away while there was a crowd in that place.*' John 5:13

'*Truly, truly, I say to you, the Son can do nothing of Himself, unless it is something He sees the Father doing; for whatever the Father does, these things the Son also does in like manner.*' John 5:19

'I can do nothing on My own initiative. I do not seek My own will but the will of Him who sent me.' John 5:30

'For I have come down from heaven, not to do My own will, but the will of Him who sent Me.' John 6:38

The humility of Jesus defeated the devil and His humility through us can do the same.

The victorious people in the Bible overcame through humility such as Moses, Joseph, Mary and David.

Numbers 12:3 says, *'Now the man Moses was very humble, more than any man on the face of the earth.'* Would it not be possible that a man who was raised under Pharaoh was humble? But true humility is only found in Christ, and Moses became humbled each time God appeared onto him.

Joseph was not very humble in his younger days. However, when meeting Pharaoh face to face, Joseph displays humility. Pharaoh tells Joseph about a dream and his need to find what it means. Joseph's response is found in Genesis 41:16, *'It is not in me; God will give Pharaoh a favorable answer.'*

Mary has just been told she has been selected to bear the Lord Jesus in her womb. What a heady experience for a young woman. Yet, her response is one of humility and obedience, as recorded in Luke 1:38 when she says, *'Behold, the bond slave of the Lord; may it be done to me according to your word.'*

David had found success on the battlefield and was immensely popular with the people of Israel. However, when given the opportunity to marry the daughter of the king, his response was one of humility. David responds to Saul in 1 Samuel 18:18, by saying *"Who am I, and what is my life or my father's family in Israel, that I should be the king's son-in-law?"*

Normally when the giants of the Bible are mentioned, they are described as overcomers, conquerors, brave in battle, bold, decisive, and self-confident. However, a major quality they had in common was humility. Otherwise the Lord could not have used them so powerfully.

It is not enough to be simply humble in our self, but to be humble in the Lord.

'He has told you, O man, what is good; and what does the Lord require of you, But to do justice, to love kindness, and to walk humbly with your God?' Micah 6:8

When we walk humbly with the Lord, we walk in a partnership in which we are not alone in our decision making, our ministry, or our personal interactions with people.

I once saw an amusing t-shirt which showed a meek little lamb confronted by roaring lions. This little lamb is walking with Jesus, hand in hand. As the lion approaches, the lamb simply points to Jesus and says, "I am with Him!"

Can I ask, "who is with you?" "Who sits on the throne of your heart?" I pray it is Jesus Christ, He is your King and Lord, for victory is found in Him.

Humility as a Weapon

Now let us take a closer look at humility, and the power of humility, as a weapon in strategic spiritual warfare.

In Hebrew the word humility means literally to tear down the wall. 2 Chronicles 7:14 could be understood as, "If My people will tear down their wall before Me." We seem to always be putting up walls around us for many reasons. Tearing down those walls are acts of humility.

My dear grandmother often gave me talks about life and love. There was a song by the Kingston Trio she really liked. In fact, she bought the album, and played "The Reverend Mr Black" many times back in 1962. It was a song about a preacher in a lumberjack town. This preacher was violently confronted by a lumberjack.

After a beating, the lumberjack stopped when the preacher sang, "You got to walk that lonesome valley, you got to walk it by yourself …" It was a song about non-violence and non-resistance.

"The Reverend Mr Black" used humility to touch the life of the lumberjack in the song. Jesus did the same. He always loved, and never gave the impression that He was better, although He is the only person that could have done so.

In the *Star Wars* movie, *Return of the Jedi*, there is a fight scene where Luke Skywalker confronts the Emperor. However, this is no ordinary fight scene. It is laced with overwhelming spiritual complexities. The real battle is not between two men, it is a battle within Luke Skywalker. The Emperor, according to some, is a symbol of the "Dark Side." His plan is to force Luke into the "Dark Side." The way to accomplish this goal is for Luke to get angry and lose control. If Luke hates, gets angry, and gives in to the dark character of evil; then the Emperor wins. In other words, if Luke wins the flesh battle, the Emperor wins the spiritual battle.

The same can be said about Jesus on the Cross. Jesus appeared to be the loser when His lifeless broken body was taken from the Cross and laid in a tomb. Of course, we know after His resurrection it was actually a great spiritual victory. It takes humility to win battles of the Spirit!

Humility in Action

Romans 12 is the relationship chapter, and demonstrates humility in action.

v3 '...*I say to everyone among you not to think more highly of himself than he ought to think...*'

v10 '...*give preference to one another in honor.*'

v16 '...*do not be haughty in mind, but associate with the lowly. Do not be wise in your own estimation.*'

I am in awe of the attitude of many Christians in the persecuted church of Moslem and Communist countries today. Visiting with those in the persecuted church is like living in the middle of the book of Acts. Not seeing great miracles and victories with power, but seeing brothers and sisters facing arrest, torture, and even death. These believers are more interested in being a witness for the Kingdom of Heaven, than living in comfort. They are more interested in obedience to Scriptures, than life itself.

Our Christian brothers and sisters facing death, show love and humility towards their enemies. Their situation is much more severe than most of us face, yet we fail to extend the same attitude of love and humility. We have much to learn about giving preference to one another. As we achieve this characteristic as a Church, we will see the Kingdom of Heaven come in power.

Pride

It is difficult to examine humility without an equal examination of pride. Let's read...

'For through the grace given to me I say to everyone among you not to think more highly of himself than he ought to think; but to think so as to have sound judgment, as God allotted to each a measure of faith.' Romans 12:3

Thinking more highly of oneself than he ought to think is certainly a good description of pride. This undercurrent that resides in many hearts, of one is more valuable than another, will lead to all kinds of problems. It can even rise to the level that one can think they are smarter than God. I could write here, as Christians we would never consciously think we are smarter than our Lord, but in all truth, the day anyone is smarter than God is the day they become God, and that's not going to happen!

But when we rely on our own selfish desires, and ignore the warning and teaching of Scriptures, we are actually saying, "We know better than God!"

We must be careful not to lift a weapon of our enemy – the devil. Pride is his weapon and all sin has its root in pride.

A look at Proverbs can further enlighten us about the dangers of Pride.

'*Pride goes before destruction, And a haughty spirit before stumbling.*' Proverbs 16:18

'*There is a way that seems right to a man, But its end is the way of death.*' Proverbs 14:12

'*Do not be wise in your own eyes.*' Proverbs 3:7

'*There are six things that the Lord hates ...haughty eyes.*'

Proverbs 6:16-17

'*Do not reprove a scoffer, or he will hate you, Reprove a wise man and he will love you. Give instruction to a wise man and he will be still wiser.*' Proverbs 9:8-9

'*Everyone who is proud in heart is an abomination to the Lord.*' Proverbs 16:5

Can I ask: How well do you accept reproof?

Most of us will answer that question with, "Good, ok, fine." Very few will say "I find it difficult!" However, I want you to think over your life about mistakes that you made. Now ask yourself... Was there anyone who advised you in such a way that if you had listened to them, the outcome would have been different? When you look back over your life and there is a common-thread of people who love you, advising you, but one still continues on the path, we must conclude the root cause of those mistakes was pride.

The Majority of people go through a stage in life of 'I know it all.' Some people realize sooner than others that there is always one smarter.

After my graduation from seminary and moving to my first

congregation, I thought I knew it all. Unfortunately, I was so full of pride I made no bones about telling everyone I knew it all. I became the pastor of a small congregation in East Texas, which had many troubles. But instead of loving the people and humbly seeking the Lord's direction, I asserted my way. If they would just do as I tell them, their problems would be solved; at least that was my thinking.

It was a disaster. It was the exact opposite of John 6:38. I came to do my will, and not the will of Him who sent me. As a result, I see now I was using the devil's weapon (pride), and the Kingdom of Heaven is never built on pride. If I had used the weapon of humility, it would have been different, and a much more pleasant experience for everyone.

I look back with much sadness and repentance over my pride. None of us can change the past but we can learn from it and act differently now. Pride prevents us from loving, for the end purpose of pride is to take. We are too busy loving ourselves, and our way of doing things.

When we walk with Jesus, there comes a place in that walk where He will require us to swap our pride for His humility. Humility is rooted in trusting the Lord, and this allows us to be free to love without an undercurrent that the person we love owes us. Humility brings the focus of our lives on Jesus, for He sits on the throne of our heart. Humility may be the most powerful weapon in the Heavenly arsenal, which can be used to bring His power into our lives, and bring glory to Jesus Christ. Let's pray this prayer…

"Lord Jesus, You are the source of all goodness, knowledge, and wisdom. I am nothing without you. Please shine the light of Your love into my heart and expose all the ways I embrace pride. Break my heart and bring true humility into my life. Give me the courage to renounce my pride and submit to Your authority, creating a desire to live in humility before You and everyone. Hide me behind Your cross, so You and You alone will get all the glory from my life. Amen."

CHAPTER 14

Reconciliation & Unity

Christian unity and reconciliation is vital to bring the fullness of Christ's love into a lost world living in darkness. The Church must demonstrate light. Jesus has commanded us to love one another, which results in unity. Our love for one another becomes a powerful weapon in spiritual warfare. Jesus said that the Church He is building will tear down the gates of hell. However, if the Church is divided; the gates of hell will not be attacked, and will continue to stand strong. A divided Church has no message for a divided world. A divided Church is not a victorious Church.

'... Jesus said to them, *...Any kingdom divided against itself is laid waste; and any city or house divided against itself will not stand.*' Matthew 12:25

Reconciliation consists equally in a change of attitude; a change from wrath to kindness, from condemnation to pardon, from rejection to acceptance. This kind of change is not possible without the power of the Holy Spirit; this kind of change, in addition provides the believer, you and I, with a powerful weapon against the powers of darkness. Wrath, condemnation, and rejection are replaced with kindness, pardon, and acceptance, a powerful combination in bringing peace and love into a relationship. When both parties adopt this kind of change, then the Holy Spirit will become activated, and wage war against the enemy.

A big problem in the world today and that is sad to write about, and not often heard now-a-days, is sin. Sin separates and divides. This separation and division existing today is preventing the Body of Christ from being one. Every war between nations, and every broken relationship between individuals, can be traced back to division.

One of the main purposes of Jesus' death on the cross was not simply to forgive sin, or remove the penalty of sin (hell), but to build a bridge called reconciliation. Successful reconciliation results in unity. One of my favorite paintings is *The Way of the Cross*, painted by Phil Saint. It shows Heaven on the far side of a canyon. On the near side is a scene of destruction. A huge cross has been placed connecting the two sides of the canyon. A throng of people are walking away from the burned out side toward Heaven. The cross becomes the bridge of life, hope, prosperity, and joy.

The cross is the bridge between us and our Heavenly Father, and should be a path of reconciliation of each other, which is often not the case. Jesus died so that we can have a relationship not only with our Heavenly Father, but to those God has called you to. The power of the cross can break down the walls of separation, which is the reason I think, when Jesus died on the cross, He did it for His Father. While it is true He died for the sins of the world, He also died so that His Father can have a personal relationship with the people He lovingly created; the people who were born in sin which prevents such a relationship. Jesus came and removed the sin problem. Now a relationship is possible.

Many churches focus on teaching that being a Christian is all about going to Heaven upon death, but the main purpose was relationship, not escapism. Jesus died so we could have a relationship with His Father, and thus hell can be missed and Heaven gained.

A certain verse which is not preached on often in churches is…

'Not everyone who says to Me, 'Lord, Lord' will enter the kingdom of heaven, but he who does the will of My Father who is in heaven

will enter. Many will say to Me on that day, 'Lord, Lord, did we not prophesy in Your name, and in Your name cast out demons, and in Your name perform many miracles?' And then I will declare to them, 'I never knew you, depart from Me, you who practice lawlessness.' Matthew 7:21-23

Jesus states here, just because you call Him Lord does not guarantee that He knows you. If we are lawlessness, we are declaring that He does not know us. For if He did... Would we be operating under lawlessness?

It must be a priority to develop a relationship with Jesus.

When the apostle Paul wrote his letters to the Church at Corinth, one of the problems he addressed was their division.

'Now I exhort you, brethren, by the name of our Lord Jesus Christ, that you all agree and that there be no divisions among you, but that you be made complete in the same mind and in the same judgment. For I have been informed concerning you, my brethren, by Chloe's people, that there are quarrels among you. Now I mean this, that each one of you is saying, 'I am of Paul,' and 'I of Apollos,' and 'I of Cephas,' and 'I of Christ.' Has Christ been divided? Paul was not crucified for you, was he? Or were you baptized in the name of Paul?' 1 Corinthians 1:10-13

'For even as the body is one and yet has many members, and all the members of the body, though they are many, are one body, so also is Christ. For by one Spirit we were all baptized into one body, whether Jews or Greeks, whether slaves or free, and we were all made to drink of one Spirit. For the body is not one member but many.' 1 Corinthians 12:12-14

'So that there may be no division in the body, but that the members may have the same care for one another. And if one member suffers, all the members suffer with it; if one member is honored, all the members rejoice with it. Now you are Christ's body, and individually members of it.' 1 Corinthians 12:25-27

'Therefore if anyone is in Christ, he is a new creature; the old things passed away; behold, new things have come. Now all these things are from God, who reconciled us to Himself through Christ and gave us the ministry of reconciliation, namely, that God was in Christ reconciling the world to Himself, not counting their trespasses against them, and He has committed to us the word of reconciliation. Therefore, we are ambassadors for Christ, as though God were making an appeal through us; we beg you on behalf of Christ, reconciled to God. He made Him who knew no sin to be sin on our behalf, so that we might become the righteousness of God in Him.' 2 Corinthians 5:17-21

Once you become born-again, we are reconciled to God, and immediately given under God, a ministry of reconciliation. A study of these passages would seem to result in an understanding that reconciliation is a top priority of the Lord. Jesus was working to bring reconciliation in everything He did while on earth. Not just His death on the cross, but every day in everything He did in life. Every person He spoke with, every miracle He performed, every healing and every teaching. The source of everything was reconciliation. Therefore, reconciliation should be a top priority in our lives.

Being in Christ, we have been allocated the position of being an ambassador for Him. In the natural, an ambassador is someone who represents his nation in maintaining a relationship with another nation. His job is to talk with, and understand, the cultural needs of the land where he is living, while at the same time representing the interests of his home nation. We are here on earth (but citizens of Heaven) to help people be reconciled. In fact, we are commanded to be active in the ministry of reconciliation.

'Pursue peace with all men, and the sanctification without which no one will see the Lord.' Hebrews 12:14

Reconciliation exists on three levels.

Firstly, we are to be reconciled to our Heavenly Father.

Secondly, we are to be reconciled to one another.

Thirdly, we are to be reconciled within ourselves.

The third condition may be the toughest to achieve.

'For while we were still helpless, at the right time Christ died for the ungodly. For one will hardly die for a righteous man; though perhaps for the good man someone would dare even to die. But God demonstrates His own love toward us, in that while we were yet sinners, Christ died for us. Much more then, having now been justified by His blood, we shall be saved from the wrath of God through Him. For if while we were enemies we were reconciled to God through the death of His Son, much more, having been reconciled, we shall be saved by His life. And not only this, but we also exult in God through our Lord Jesus Christ, through whom we have now received the reconciliation.' Romans 5:6-11

Jesus initiated the act of reconciliation. We do not have an excuse if we say we should only help those who want help. We must be salt and light to a dark world. Christians must demonstrate unity and reconciliation as role models to the world. Jesus prayed that His people would be one on the night that he was betrayed and arrested.

'I do not ask on behalf of these alone, but for those also who believe in Me through their word, that they may all be one, even as You, Father, are in Me and I in You, that they also may be in Us, so that the world may believe that You sent Me. The glory which You have given Me I have given to them, that they may be one, just as We are one. I in them and You in Me, that they may be perfected in unity, so that the world may know that You sent Me, and loved them, even as You have loved Me.' John 17:20-23

Our reconciliation within the body of Christ, then, is a witness of our unity, showing the world that Jesus and the Kingdom of Heaven are real. Furthermore – All people will know we are His disciples if we have love for one another. Jesus, Himself said ...

'A new commandment I give to you, that you love one another, even as I have loved you, that you also love one another. By this all men will know that you are My disciples, if you have love for one another.' John 13:34-35

We are Perfected in Unity

'But to each one of us grace was given according to the measure of Christ's gift. Therefore it says, "When He ascended on high, He led captive a host of captives, and He gave gifts to men (now this expression, "He ascended," what does it mean except that He also had descended into the lower parts of the earth? He who descended is Himself also He who ascended far above all the heavens, so that He might fill all things.) And He gave some as apostles, and some as prophets, and some as evangelists, and some as pastors and teachers for the equipping of the saints for the work of service, to the building up of the body of Christ until we all attain to the unity of the faith, and of the knowledge of the Son of God, to a mature man, to the measure of the stature which belongs to the fullness of Christ. As a result, we are no longer to be children, tossed here and there by waves and carried about by every wind of doctrine, by the trickery of men, by craftiness in deceitful scheming but speaking the truth in love, we are to grow up in all aspects into Him who is the head, even Christ from whom the whole body, being fitted and held together with the Lord, that you walk no longer just as the Gentiles also walk, in the futility of their mind.' Ephesians 4:7-17

The purpose of those in ministry is to bring unity, and where you see a believer or church seeking unity, it is the sign of spiritual maturity. In Ephesians 4:13, Paul expands on how unity will, and must happen, before Jesus returns. Jesus will return for a pure, spotless bride at peace within herself. Paul writes here that we *all* attain to unity, not just some of us. The whole Church will have the knowledge of Jesus. We will all know Him (have a relationship with him). The Church will then develop a maturity, which comes with the fullness of a wholesome healthy relationship in Christ.

This maturity will result in an infilling of the Holy Spirit, which will allow the body of Christ to march in powerful victories. It will also strengthen the Church for the promised persecution ahead. Unity is vital because the challenges facing the suffering Church are severe and grim. With each challenge comes opportunity, and a united Body of Christ will seize each opportunity to bring glory to Jesus Christ. We are all part of the body of Christ (1 Corinthians 12) and are joined to other parts. As we each fulfill our role, and connect to others doing theirs; the Body of Christ functions as it should.

'So, as those who have been chosen of God, holy and beloved, put on a heart of compassion, kindness, humility, gentleness and patience; bearing with one another, and forgiving each other, whoever has a complaint against anyone; just as the Lord forgave you, so also should you. Beyond all these things put on love, which is the perfect bond of unity. Let the peace of Christ rule in your hearts, to which indeed you were called in one body; and be thankful.' Colossians 3:12-15

As we develop proper mature Christian character we will bear with one another, and forgive one another, because unity creates peace and purpose. King David wrote, '...how good and how pleasant it is for brothers to dwell together in unity.' Psalm 133:1

What does all of this have to do with spiritual warfare?

When I was in the Army going through my basic training, one dreadful day was spent digging a foxhole. Our platoon was assigned an area, and told we could expect an attack in the evening. So, we had all day to make continual improvements on our defensive position. We were told to take the dirt and pile it up directly in front of our foxhole. My comrade and I would dig and dig, in-fact we dug all day. Why? Because we knew an attack was coming.

Our mission was to protect the rest of our comrades by shooting the enemy advancing on them, and our comrade's mission was to shoot any enemy advancing on me and my partner in the foxhole. The whole platoon had to be in unity, to be able to protect each other, and therefore, be successful in our defense against the enemy attack.

Perhaps the devil's biggest weapon is using Christians to create and keep division. Let us consider Ephesians 6. Paul writes regarding the armor of God. Even in a quick study of this portion of Scripture, you can notice the back of the soldier is not protected! This would imply we are to protect one another's back, and therefore we need to ask, are we doing this for our fellow Christian? Or do we fall at the hurdle of gossip by stabbing them in the back? We must become answerable for our actions!

Remember this quote…

"In essentials, we have unity.
In non-essentials, we have diversity.
In all things, we have love."

This little quote sounds nice until you start to live it in the real world. What are the essentials? There is vast disagreement. I once preached a series on "the essentials." Afterward, there were those who protested that I did not include their pet doctrine. Others told me something I thought was essential did not matter one way or the other to them. We Christians have a wide span of opinions, which are constantly changing. In fact, if I were to preach the same series today, I am sure it would be different. Topics chosen then may be deleted, and other topics not considered then, may be selected.

There are no easy answers. When do we seek to "agree to disagree?" At what point, do we seek compromises? In fact, just using the word, "compromise", can get many Christians upset because they will "never compromise with the world."

Sometimes it is difficult, near impossible, to get local ministers to participate together. In the past few months I have had to seek the

Lord about the whole issue of Christian unity. I have been taught how certain groups who worship Jesus are wrong because of some doctrinal differences. These groups such as Jehovah Witnesses and Mormons have many beliefs with which I do not agree with. But at what point are we to say that they are wrong? After all, there are beliefs that Baptists have, that I do not agree with. And there are beliefs that Methodist have, that I do not agree with. In fact there are beliefs I held twenty years ago that I do no longer agree with today. What does this show me? I am constantly growing, constantly coming to the Light, and as I do, He shows me where to change!

When does agreeing to disagree become the best approach? When does it come to the time when we must break fellowship? How do we break fellowship without creating more heartache, anger, and bitterness? There is certainly no easy answer

When we look at the followers of Jesus, it will show great diversity. Certainly, a tax collector such as Matthew, will not have a warm, fuzzy relationship with a zealot like Simon. But both were apostles who Jesus called to walk with Him. Unity obviously does not mean 100% agreement on everything, but it does mean unity of heart. Unity of heart is where we seek the best for the other person, and this must never be forsaken.

Unity is vital.

We must take note that unity is vital...

1 - A jealousy-ridden Church cannot reach a jealousy-ridden world.

2 - A selfish, greedy Church cannot reach a selfish, greedy world.

If we function together in love and unity, we will generate God's love. Any attempt for the devil to compromise our message will fail. The devil's attacks on a part of the body will result in greater compassion from the other parts of the body. Instead of us judging our brothers and sisters, we will seek only the best for them.

To achieve unity in the Church, loyalty is a necessity. Webster's Dictionary describes loyalty as: faithful to commitments or obligations. Here are some interesting and vital Scriptures about Loyalty.

'*Many a man proclaims his own loyalty, but who can find a trustworthy man.*' Proverbs 20:6

'*Loyalty and truth preserve the king, and he upholds his throne by righteousness.*' Proverbs 20:28

'*He who pursues righteousness and loyalty finds life, righteousness and honor.*' Proverbs 21:21

'*What shall I do with you, O Ephraim? What shall I do with you, O Judah? For your loyalty is like a morning cloud and like the dew which goes away early. Therefore, I have hewn them in pieces by the prophets, I have slain them by the words of My mouth; and the judgments on you are like the light that goes forth. For I delight in loyalty rather than sacrifice, and in the knowledge of God rather than burnt offerings. But like Adam they have transgressed the covenant; there they have dealt treacherously against Me.*' Hosea 6:4-7

The Bible describes loyalty with words such as life, honor, righteousness, trustworthy, and truth. Described by Paul, the Church is the body of Christ in 1 Corinthians 12. It is one living organism with much diversity, having Jesus as the highest common denominator.

3 - Unity is a witness in our efforts for peace-making.

Jesus said, '*Blessed are the peacemakers, for they shall be called sons of God.*' Matthew 5:9

Dear reader, it is vital for believers to work together for unity and reconciliation.

In our walk towards unity, the most essential thing is Jesus Christ. Everything else can be a non-essential. We can allow diversity on mode of Baptism, different viewpoints about Communion, speaking in tongues, role of women in the church, and countless other issues the church struggles with each day. What is important is for Christians to come together, at the foot of the Cross, in Christ. The Church has the power to establish the Kingdom of Heaven, in which the gates of hell will not prevail against us, because unity is in our midst.

4 - The Unity of the Body of Christ is a condition for the return of Jesus. (This is explained more fully in the chapter on intercessory prayer). The Church will become as pure as the bride of Christ for His return. We must remember that Jesus is coming back for a pure bride, not a bride who is divided and in conflict within herself.

Unity is a weapon.

While there are similarities between unity and reconciliation, they are different. Reconciliation assumes a broken relationship which needs healing, and results in unity. However, there are examples of disunity, where broken relationships do not exist, such as when two groups are seeking a similar ministry in the same city, unaware that the other exists. In fact, there is no relationship. And therefore, Christian relationships must be developed and cultivated.

Jesus prays prior to His arrest...

'I do not ask on behalf of these alone, but for those also who believe in Me though their word, that they may all be one; even as You, Father, are in Me and I in You, that they also may be in Us, so that the world may believe that You sent Me. The Glory which You have given Me I have given to them, that they may be one, just as We are one. I (Jesus) in them and You (the Father) in Me, that they may be perfected in unity, so that the world may know that You sent Me, and loved them, even as You have loved me.' John 17:20-23

I am reminded of a cartoon where it showed people sitting at a dinner table with lovely stew in a bowl that had been served to them. However, they had a problem! They were struggling to eat the stew due to the spoons having extremely long handles. Each time they would try and feed themselves, they basically could not put the spoon into their mouth. It was only when one person realized that for him to be fed, he had to feed another, and in turn the other person had to feed him.

Unity of the Spirit is helping each other move that one step more!

Cycle of Reconciliation

There is a cycle of reconciliation which helps us to understand the challenges and steps needed to bring success as we seek to be peacemakers and establish a renewal of relationships with those divided. This cycle of reconciliation is:

1. Relationship
2. Injury
3. Withdrawal
4. Reclaiming identity - a new mindset -
5. Internal commitment to reconciliation
6. Restoration of risk
7. Negotiate - establish needs which are to be met

1. Relationship.

This is the starting point. Two people, groups, or nations are in a relationship. It may not necessarily be a good relationship but they know each other, and have a reasonable peaceful co-existence.

2. Injury.

One party, or perhaps both, say or do something which causes injury. It could be something simple, such as gossip between people, up to and including invasion with an army who conquers a nation, killing many people, and taking away basic human rights.

3. Withdrawal.

The hurt party (and sometimes this is both parties) seek security and safety away from the other party.

4. Reclaiming identity.

A new mind-set must develop. There needs to be a building of positive self-image. One party may have been treated badly, and needs to reject the idea that "I am bad." Or, it may have been that the guilty party feels ashamed of their actions and attitudes. In many ways, both sides need to reclaim a new identity.

It is worth noting that when Britain withdrew its sovereignty from the 26 counties in Ireland, forming the Republic of Ireland. The flag of the Republic the tricolor, was designed Green, White, and Orange, and is symbolic of the two groups of people making up Ireland. The Green is for the Catholic, native Irish, while the Orange represents the Protestant who moved into Ireland long ago from England, Scotland, and Wales with King William of Orange. The white is symbolic of the peace which is desired between these groups. Those who made the flag did so in hope to see unity come to their land, as both sides work together for the common good.

5. Internal commitment to reconciliation.

Before anyone can make outward changes, there must be an internal change. Those who have been hurt and still carry anger with bitterness must reach a point in their heart where they are not only willing, but committed to, finding a solution and that is found in Christ. True reconciliation comes from everyone seeking resolution for the difficulties.

6. Restoration of risk.

Even after a group gains their self-respect, and makes an internal commitment for peace, it can still be risky to take the first step. There is much uncertainty involved in reaching out to someone who has been hurt, to seek peace, harmony, and ultimate unity.

7. Negotiate.

Establish needs which are to be met. The negotiation process allows each injured party to view the "other side" as human beings with much in common. As each party can spend time in an open attempt to understand, it brings great insight.

A friend once told me of his summer job in Belfast. He grew up as a Protestant with no contact with anyone who might have been Catholic. He got a summer job working with the parks department, and his first assignment was to rake leaves on a team with four other teenage boys.

As they worked they talked together, it was then he found out that the other four were Catholics. After the second day at work, he realized they were all alike. They liked the same music, went to the same movies, and even had the same frustrations with their girlfriends.

His past had kept him separated, but getting to know each other brought understanding, healing, and reconciliation.

The Church is in a unique and wonderful position to make a difference in a world which faces increased confusion and division between individuals and groups.

As we have a powerful partner in the Prince of Peace, our Lord Jesus Christ. We must never retreat from the chance to be peacemakers and bring reconciliation to the world we live in.

CHAPTER 15

Spiritual Gifts

The Baptism in the Holy Spirit and "the gifts" of the Holy Spirit which were given to unify the Church, in some instances, either through ignorance or pride of people, have made them divisive in the Body of Christ.

Many seek "the gifts" for their own popularity to be today's Christian stardom. Yet, our priority is not pursued of gifts, but pursued of the Giver, Jesus Christ.

'And without faith it is impossible to please Him, for he who comes to God must believe that He is and that He is a rewarder of those who seek Him.' Hebrews 11:6

One could interpret this verse as, "I want the gifts. I want prosperity. I want earthly blessings, as Jesus will reward me for seeking Him." A closer look will show that the reward is the greatest reward one can have - Jesus Himself! If we seek only Jesus, then the reward is Jesus! If we seek only the gifts, then we will be unbalanced, which could lead to a path resulting in self-glorification. When we allow "experience" to determine our gauge, then we are placing experience over Scripture.

If someone allows an experience to take priority over Scripture, there is a danger that Scripture can be deemed optional, and a fanaticism may prevail.

God's Word must be our spiritual ruler. We must allow His Word to have the final authority, not hearsay or part truth.

There are 15 spiritual gifts listed in Romans 12 and 1 Corinthians 12. They are service, teaching, exhortation, giving, leadership, mercy, wisdom, knowledge, faith, healing, miracles, distinguishing of spirits, tongues, interpretation of tongues, and prophecy. These are some but not all of the gifts of the Holy Spirit. Much is written in the Bible of the Holy Spirit and power.

'*This is the One (Jesus) who baptizes in the Holy Spirit.*' John 1:33

'*He (Jesus) will baptize you with the Holy Spirit and fire.*' Matthew 3:11

Jesus said, '*But when He, the Spirit of Truth, comes, He will guide you into all the truth; for He will not speak on His own initiative, but whatever He hears, He will speak; and He will disclose to you what is to come. He will glorify Me.*' John 16:13-14

'*Gathering them (His followers) together, He (Jesus) commanded them not to leave Jerusalem, but to wait for what the Father had promised, which, He said, 'you heard of from Me; for John baptized with water, but you will be baptized with the Holy Spirit not many days from now.*' Acts 1:4-5

'*And they were all filled with the Holy Spirit.*' Acts 2:4

It is no accident that Paul speaks of the Church as a diverse body prior to his teaching on spiritual gifts in 1 Corinthians 12. He also encourages Christians to earnestly seek spiritual gifts in 1 Corinthians 12; 31, and again in 1 Corinthians 14:1. The original text is, '*Be chasing the love, be-boiling yet the spirituals, rather yet ye may be before prophesying.*' (Greek Interlinear Bible)

Within the context of love, we are to seek after the spiritual gifts. With the difficulties between Christians over spiritual gifts, it is easy to understand why the Holy Spirit guided the apostle Paul to include an exposé on love.

When spiritual gifts are used to glorify Jesus with a humble and grateful attitude, the Holy Spirit manifests himself and moves with power.

Without going into an exhaustive examination of each of the 15 spiritual gifts listed above, or the other gifts listed individually in Scripture, we want to understand how spiritual gifts can be used as weapons in our spiritual warfare.

There are gifts such as used by Bezalel to help built the tabernacle. Not all spiritual gifts would be classified as supernatural in the same way as speaking in tongues. Bezalel was a skilled craftsman with the Spirit of God in wisdom.

'Now the Lord spoke to Moses, saying, 'See I have called by name Bezalel, the son of Uri, the son of Hur, of the tribe of Judah. I have filled him with the Spirit of God in wisdom, in understanding, in knowledge, and in all kinds of craftsmanship, to make artistic designs, for work in gold, in silver, and the bronze, and in the cutting of stones for settings, and in the carving of wood, that he may work in all kinds of craftsmanship.' Exodus 31:1-5

Every Christian has spiritual gifts to exercise and use. Your gift is an act of obedience (another weapon of strategic spiritual warfare). Therefore, we need to understand that gifts are not just for leaders or those with special talents, but for everyone. As the Church, being the complete body of Christ, moves in the Holy Spirit, each member should be moving in their individual gifting, then the Church will really be functioning as the Church, winning victories, and seeing the Kingdom of Heaven manifest on the earth.

Because spiritual gifts are to glorify Jesus, many spiritual gifts have an opposite spirit which can be used to defeat the demonic spirit.

Loren Cunningham, founder of *Youth with a Mission*, has

built much ministry on the theme of "Coming in the Opposite Spirit." For example, when there is a selfish spirit present from the devil, we can exercise a giving Spirit and gift. When there is a spirit of despair present, we can exercise a Spirit and gift of exhortation. When there is a spirit of disbelief present, we can exercise the gift and Spirit of Faith. The list is never ending. Whatever the devil brings into our lives, we can bring the Truth and Power of the Holy Spirit which is the opposite.

Gift of Speaking in Tongues

Praying in tongues can be a great weapon. Firstly, it is born of the Spirit into your life, and secondly, it is the Spirit praying through us, by-passing our minds.

Some people have set aside one hour a day to pray in tongues. This comes down to a love relationship with God, and discipline of the flesh. For as you enter the realm of tongues, you are allowing The Holy Spirit to speak through you, to pray what He wants and not what you would want. In turn this strengthens our own Spirit, drawing us close to the Lord, and His plan for our life.

Scripture teaches…

'…the Spirit Himself intercedes for us with groaning too deep for words; and He who searches the hearts knows what the mind of the Spirit is, because He intercedes for the saints according to the will of God.' Romans 8:26-27

Those with a prayer language can pray almost anytime, anyplace, silently and privately without drawing attention to themselves. This truly addresses the forces of darkness around them while inviting Jesus into the situation. Proper private prayer will not draw attention in any way to the one praying. Some people privately pray in tongues during various worship services in congregations which do not practice tongues, nor approve of their use.

Gift of Knowledge

One of the least spoken about, yet one of the most valuable spiritual gifts, is the Gift of Knowledge. Jesus demonstrated His gift of knowledge while speaking with the woman at the well.

'The woman said to him (Jesus), 'Sir, give me this water, so I will not be thirsty nor come all the way here to draw.' He (Jesus) said to her, 'Go, call your husband and come here. The woman answered and said, 'I have no husband.' Jesus said to her, 'You have correctly said, 'I have no husband'; for you have had five husbands and the one whom you now have is not your husband; this you have said truly.' John 4:15-18

Elisha demonstrated the gift of Knowledge after his servant Gehazi secretly went to Naaman, and deceived him into giving a reward when the Lord healed Naaman of leprosy.

'But he (Gehazi) went in and stood before his master. And Elisha said to him, 'Where have you been, Gehazi?' And he said, 'Your servant went nowhere.' Then he said to him, 'Did not my heart go with you, when the man turned from his chariot to meet you? Is it a time to receive money and to receive clothes and olive groves and vineyards and sheep and oxen and male and female servants? Therefore, the leprosy of Naaman shall cling to you and to your descendants forever.' So he went out from his presence a leper as white as snow.' 2 Kings 5:25-27

The Christian with the gift of Knowledge will learn facts supernaturally, directly from the Lord, rather than from any Earthly source. It is a gift requiring great humility to be effective. The Lord does not simply drop a fact into the mind of a person; it is the result of a deep commitment and close personal relationship between a believer and Jesus. For instance, Daniel is a good example. King Nebuchadnezzar had a dream and forgot it. He wanted his wise men to tell him the dream and the interpretation. Daniel went to the king with powerful words.

'Daniel answered the king and said, 'As for the mystery about which the king has inquired, neither wise men, conjurers, magicians nor diviners are able to declare it to the king. However, there is a God in heaven who reveals mysteries, and He has made known to King Nebuchadnezzar what will take place in the latter days.' Daniel 2:27-28

Like all "gifts" of the Spirit, one must firstly sense in the Spirit, direction and then timing. Who is the gift for? And what is the gift? Also, as important; is the timing and how to deliver the 'gift.'

Imagine you having been told to attend a gathering and present a gift to a special person. Would you not need to know some things to maximize the moment? Who is the gift for? What is the gift? (If it's big do you need a trailer etc?) And at what point do you want the gift presented?

Those 3 areas will make the gift have a greater impact. And as it is in the natural, so is it in the Spirit.

Ask Jesus, what is the gift? Who is it for? And when to give it? Watch God demonstrate His love manifested through understanding!

Gift of Discerning of Spirits

Jesus said, *'See to it that no one misleads you. For many will come in My name, saying, I am the Christ,' and will mislead many.'* Matthew 24:4-5

We live in a time when the nature of the world, and its sin, has infiltrated the church. Church doctrines and policies are being reshaped. Scriptures are taken out of context, all for the whosoever to attain peoples approval on what God calls sin.

For example; homosexuality, living together, and same-sex marriages have gained a momentum with government backing. Governments are now forcing churches to close, except if they adopt these anti-Bible practices. In certain states in the USA, the government has removed charity status from churches when they are unwilling to conform. It's only a matter of time before this same ruling will apply in the UK.

Like all "gifts" of the Spirit, the evidence is not about what you see or hear from a natural sense, but from spiritual senses. If it was only natural, a non-Spirit-filled person could discern the same. But it is the Spirit given knowledge that gives us an advantage if we listen. And as time closes in on the earth, it is only a matter of time before we will have to pay with our lives for standing with Jesus against the darkness.

I believe this was my gift during the days of the Goeppingen, Germany, Chapel fellowship. When I sensed demonic forces had infiltrated our time together as a group, immediately we prayed for the Lord to fill the room with His Spirit and drive the darkness away. It was joyful and liberating to feel the atmosphere changed.

Discernment of Spirits is a gift which seems to be more active in women than men. It could be that women are more sensitive and therefore more easily sense a move of the Spirit, but one thing is for sure. Whether you are male or female, God is seeking to manifest His gift through you.

Through the gifts, the Church will gain the long-term victory over the devil as we work together as a body. This is because each member will exercise their gift, and when everyone is flowing in the Holy Spirit, making their contribution, seeking the Lord and His glory; it can be compared to a motor running on all cylinders. This motor will be in operation, destroying the gates of hell.

CHAPTER 16

Forgiveness

When bitter things take place in our life like; divorce, loss of a job, death, or accident. Our hearts can become filled with hate, bitterness, and desire for revenge. Those are not the traits which Jesus had, or neither should we have them. But we must forgive! I am not saying forgiveness is easy, nor it is done without cost nor sacrifice. Those who refuse to forgive often have deep hurt, which needs time and supernatural healing. However, most of our stubbornness to not forgive, concerns hurt, which can have a side effect.

One example in my life when I felt anger and bitterness concerned a job opportunity which went to someone else. I was employed in a certain position, when a job in my company, that I had all the qualifications for, became available, and what also was good, it would give me a chance to witness for Jesus.

I submitted my application, was selected for the interviews, and I eagerly met with the committee who would make the decision. I felt confident about being the best candidate with the best qualifications, education, and experience. But, the company had other plans. The company was going to close another depot, and made the decision to transfer the man in that position there, to this new position that I was applying for.

Boy, was I mad. I was bitter. I felt so betrayed by the company. I resented the new man, and avoided him whenever possible. He even came looking for me once and it took him a while to find me. He wanted me to help him, and I did not want to help him, but I was wrong.

Years later, after much thought and prayer, I knew that if I had gotten the job, I would likely have stayed there in Orlando, Florida, and missed out on the plan Jesus had for my life.

Through a complex web of job changes, promotions, disappointments, new opportunities, and professional contacts; the Lord has opened new doors of exciting ministry which have been better. If I had known then what I know now; I would never have even applied for that position.

In the past ten years since someone else was selected, I have had ministry in areas of the company, then working overseas as a missionary. Later I became a pastor of one of the most amazing congregations anywhere. It is truly a dream come true to be at Faith United Methodist Church in Bowling Green, KY.

None of this would have been possible if I had gotten the job. So, when I was bitter, angry, and upset; I should have calmed down and listened to the Lord. Sometimes it is difficult to forgive because our ego, pride, and selfish desires get in the way.

I forgot that it is not about me, it is about Jesus. Unforgiveness is a weapon of destruction. It is a tool of the devil to create division in the body of Christ, and bondage for the Christian who is embracing it. Too many Christians are bound to hatred, bitterness, anger, resentment, and mistrust because of the unwillingness to forgive.

We need to never forget one basic truth, our Christian life, which includes the need to forgive, is not about any human being. It is about the honor of Jesus Christ. It is neither about you nor me, it is solely about Jesus. And as we honor Jesus by putting Him first, we will be a witness for good.

As we continue our examination of strategic spiritual warfare, and weapons given to us as we fight the powers of darkness, the power of forgiveness can make a difference.

It is easy to understand the power of unforgiveness.

In our on-going look at weapons of strategic spiritual warfare, those divinely powerful weapons designed to tear down strongholds of darkness; it is easy to see the power of forgiveness. Forgiveness paves the way for reconciliation and unity. And as a result, there will be strong efforts to prevent us from forgiving those who have harmed and disappointed us. We must always be on our guard against those spiritual forces of wickedness who try to keep us from loving the way Jesus loves. It is interesting to learn how well known and popular Christians face the same trials.

For example, Corrie Ten Boom, a Dutch woman whose family helped the Jews escape from the Nazis in World War II, was imprisoned in Ravensbruck concentration camp. After the war, she wrote several books and in one of them she tells about how she shared her testimony at a gathering in Germany. After the meeting, she noticed a man. This man was a man that she would never forget because he was one of the officers at Ravensbruck. She could see him walking around the camp with a smug look on his face and leather whip in his hand, which he used liberally. Her heart burned with hatred as all the horrible memories of those days flooded into her mind. The death of her sister, Betsy, and the shame of parading naked in front of those male officers, brought feelings of rage. Did this man remember her?

Most of the people in attendance were gathering their coats and heading for the exits. But this man was walking toward her! Corrie looked away and picked up her purse. He was coming straight for her. She took a step toward the exit when they were face to face. He smiled and told her that it was a wonderful feeling to know that Jesus forgives sins. He went on to tell her he was now a Christian and that all the terrible things he did were forgiven. He told her about his repentance from the sins committed while an officer at Ravensbruck. He then stuck out his hand to her, and asked for her to forgive him also.

The last thing Corrie Ten Boom wanted to do was to forgive the man who caused her such deep, indescribable pain. In the few seconds standing there, she realized the cost Jesus paid to provide her forgiveness. It was her sin which Jesus went to the cross to forgive. But these thoughts still did not create any desire to forgive this man. She finally asked the Lord to provide. She took his hand and immediately felt a tingle go down her arm and into her hand. Then a rush of love came to her and she could then forgive him honestly, and with a pure heart.

The power of the Holy Spirit was released for all to see. The witness of her forgiveness may have touched many hearts beyond any of the words she spoke to the group. Yes, forgiveness is a powerful spiritual weapon.

If other Christians can forgive, and not respond with anger or bitterness in a life and death struggle, why do Christians refuse to forgive over small everyday mistakes which are likely to be forgotten in a week?

We forgive and the Holy Spirit moves in such a way so that the lost have a witness. People bound in hatred and bitterness see the hope which comes from forgiveness. There is a release in the hearts of men as Jesus reaches out through our forgiveness of one another, and the power of His love takes over their hearts.

It probably will not happen immediately, but this is the way of strategic spiritual warfare. The powerful weapon of forgiveness allows the Holy Spirit to hover around those watching, and seeds are planted. As those seeds are watered by other ministers of His truth; eventually the battle for their heart is won. Forgiveness provides the Holy Spirit opportunity to change lives.

Other weapons in our warfare include unity and reconciliation. Forgiveness makes unity and reconciliation possible. As Christians forgive one another, work together for the Kingdom of Heaven, and create an atmosphere of reconciliation; it all connects and works together to form a power, resulting in the total defeat of the devil.

As we examine the power of forgiveness, it is a reminder that we are in spiritual warfare. The enemy is not flesh and blood, but spiritual forces of wickedness. Our weapons are divinely powerful for the destruction of fortresses. Forgiveness is one of these weapons.

As we look past the person who has harmed us, we see the real enemy, which is the spiritual powers of darkness. The devil who wants to see us angry, bitter, fearful, and prideful is active, to pull our attention from Jesus, to our situation. If we want to walk in spiritual power and victory, forgiveness is a must in our life.

Forgiveness is not just about us, it is about honoring Jesus, as He forgave, so it is for us to forgive also!

CHAPTER 17

Sacraments

Most evangelical denominations observe two ordinances; Baptism and the Lord's Supper. These are viewed as ordinances and observed because Jesus told us to do them

'Go therefore and make disciples of all the nations, baptizing them in the Name of the Father, and the Son and the Holy Spirit.' Matthew 28:19

'And when He (Jesus) had taken some bread and had given thanks, He broke it and gave it to them, saying, 'This is my body which is given for you; do this in remembrance of Me.' Luke 22:19

Many mainline traditional denominations and especially the Roman Catholic churches, observe sacraments. A Sacrament is an act done on earth which stimulates or energizes the Holy Spirit. Not only are these acts done because Jesus told us to do them, but going a step further, His presence is there as we do.

The groups who observe sacraments recognize seven of them. They are Baptism, Eucharist (also known as Communion, Lord's Supper and Last Supper), Confirmation, Penance (also known as Confession), Extreme unction (also known as Anointing of the Sick), Holy Orders (also known as Ordination), and Matrimony (also known as Wedding or Marriage).

I searched for a good description or definition of Sacrament without finding one, so I decided to give my own. I think a Sacrament can be properly illustrated as an action which invites the presence and power of The Holy Spirit into our lives, and the lives of those involved. Sacraments are also weapons of strategic spiritual warfare. Remembering strategy is a long-term action in preparation for the needs of the future, the proper practice of sacraments will bring spiritual power into our lives for the long term.

I really believe as sacraments are practiced sincerely, and in the fear of the Lord, the Holy Spirit is energized. The Lord honors the practice of the sacraments, and uses them to seal the believer in His grace. Because the Holy Spirit is roused to activity, this brings a power over the Christians who are participating in the sacrament. Also, the power of the Holy Spirit will drive away any demonic influence, and bind the intentions of hell for harm.

In many ways sacraments are mysterious for those unaccustomed to their power. It is a shame that more sacraments are not practiced nor celebrated by all of the church. I fear the divide between Protestant and Catholic prevents an honest examination and embrace of sacraments. Paul writes to the Church in Ephesus and speaks about a part of the mystery of His plan.

'To me, the very least of all saints, this grace was given, to preach to the Gentiles the unfathomable riches of Christ and to bring to light what is the administration of the mystery which for ages had been hidden in God who created all things so that the manifold wisdom of God might now be made known through the church to the rulers and the authorities in the heavenly places. This was in accordance with the eternal purpose which He carried out in Christ Jesus our Lord.' Ephesians 3:8-11

Mystery needs a bit of explanation. Often mystery is thought of in terms of a "who done it?" Perry Mason and Agatha Christie are murder mysteries. When the New Testament writers tell of mystery, they are explaining there were plans and purposes of

God which were kept hidden until Jesus came. The establishment of sacraments, and the use of sacraments to invoke the power of the Holy Spirit is one such mystery. Prior to the coming of Jesus, these weapons of strategic spiritual warfare were not available for the people of God.

Baptism

Baptism is a washing. In fact, baptism is one of only a few Greek words which were not translated into English when the Bible became available in other languages. Baptism is from the Greek term "baptizo" which means to plunge into the water and wash. Women of those days would "baptizo" their clothes at the creek. It is easy to visualize the early Church going to the river as new converts would be plunged into the water and their sins washed away.

The Church uses clean water when Baptisms are performed in the sanctuary. But Baptism is more than merely getting someone wet; it is symbolic of a spiritual cleansing as well. Baptism frees a person from the sins, and bondage of the past, allowing him to enter a new and supernatural life under the Lordship of Jesus Christ. When Baptism is celebrated in a river, creek or a stream, there is a symbolic removal of sin, as it is removed from his life and flows downstream away, and out of his life forever.

When the recipient humbly and sincerely enters Baptism in obedience to the call of Christ, the Holy Spirit is present to work supernaturally. I remember testimonies from people who were healed of lifelong diseases at their Baptism. I also have heard testimonies of deliverance from long term addictions at Baptism. Also, it is possible for a person to be Baptized in the Holy Spirit at the moment of their water Baptism.

Baptism is a new beginning. Every new beginning in Christ, such as Marriage, and Ordination, is an opportunity for the Holy

Spirit to bring a sealing of His presence and power, which will remain for all eternity.

Eucharist

We may sing, "Be present at our table", as the bread and cup are taken in Holy Communion, when actually; we are present at His table. One truly sad observation about the Christian faith is how divisive Communion has become. Some will not partake unless an ordained minister from their denomination is leading the worship. Others will not partake if someone they do not agree with is at the same table. And of course, there are those who practice "closed Communion," where only members which the elders have picked from the congregation are allowed to join the celebration of Christ's death and resurrection. The devil has attacked the Eucharist because he knows the power of Communion when observed properly.

Since the Lord's Supper is at the Lord's Table, we do not have the authority to prevent anyone from participating, and every Christian is invited by Jesus to "come and dine." We cannot refuse His invitation and expect to continue to walk with His blessing.

To understand how Communion is a sacrament may be the easiest of all those examined in this chapter, because we can see, touch, and even taste the presence of Jesus in the bread and cup. The body of Christ was broken and the bread we hold was broken. His body was broken so our brokenness can be healed. His blood was shed and we can see the dark juice in the cup. His blood provides forgiveness of sins. Our brokenness is healed, and our sins are forgiven. This is why we celebrate Communion.

And as we come to His table with humility and an eagerness to draw close to Jesus, He is there. The Holy Spirit is present to flood us with power, purpose, and the Love of Jesus. Therefore, we should come boldly and joyfully to the table of the Lord, to receive all Jesus has for us.

Confirmation

For denominations, which practice infant Baptism, there is a rite of passage known as Confirmation. Confirmation is a planned worship service in which young people, usually around 8-10 years of age, make a profession of faith, and are granted membership in the congregation.

In Judaism, a boy celebrates Bar Mitzvah at the age of 13. Many Christians may think a Bar Mitzvah is only a ceremony, like one we have seen on a TV show, and at the end, the "boy" proudly proclaims, "Today I am a man."

While in fact, many Bar Mitzvah rituals include a humorous statement of thanksgiving by the father, because he is no longer responsible for the sins of his son; it is an acknowledgment of personal responsibility and maturity. The ceremony is not a "graduation," marking the ending of childhood and a declaration of manhood, because religious training continues. It is a positive passing point in which a young man makes a commitment to grow in his faith.

The Christian Confirmation process is usually a series of classes led by a pastor, priest, or a leading teacher for a group of a particular age. The Confirmation ceremony is then a time when these young people make a public profession of faith, followed in some cases by a prayer from a Bishop as he lays hands on those being confirmed. Then, they participate in their "first Communion."

For denominations, which do not practice infant Baptism, I notice a similar mindset. Young people need a planned opportunity to understand the basics of the Christian faith, make a profession of faith, and celebrate Baptism. As a Protestant Pastor, I have led many "pastor's classes" prior to Easter, with the intent of sharing the Gospel message with young people. I would tell them what it means to be a Christian and what it means to be a member of the

Church. Many of these young people would make a commitment of their life to Jesus, make a confession of faith, and were baptized on Easter Sunday.

We have looked at three different, yet similar situations, in which young people are making commitments to God. I believe it is vitally important to teach and encourage pre-teens about Jesus. As it is done Biblically and as everyone seeks the Spirit of God to participate, this Sacrament provides eternal divine protection for those being confirmed. I am not saying they are automatically saved because of a ceremony and/or they repeated words; but the Lord will honor the childlike faith of a sincere profession.

It is important for the church, pastors, and parents to continue the practice of purposefully presenting the Gospel to pre-teens and do everything we can to encourage a lifelong relationship with Jesus. If we do this properly and Biblically, we are engaging in a Sacrament and the Holy Spirit will be active to give permanence to the work of our hands.

'Let the favor of the Lord our God be upon us; and confirm for us the work of our hands...' Psalm 90:17

Confession

As Christians, we know we are not sinless, although we should sin less. Because we continue to fall short of the glory of God, the Bible speaks of ways to overcome sin and regain the fullness of our personal relationship with Jesus. There is a need for constant repentance. And proper repentance requires confession.

Again, we can look at the Catholic Church and the confessional, where a priest is behind a curtain, and parishioners enter to "make confession." But confession does not need such formality, nor an ordained priest.

'If we confess our sins, He is faithful and righteous to forgive us our sins and to cleanse us from all unrighteousness.' 1 John 1:9

Some churches will hold public confessions when a leader has broken the church rules and is seeking to be welcomed back into fellowship. However, public confession is seldom effective, and can be very damaging in many ways, as it normally exposes one party but not the other. And as Jesus said, "*he who is without sin among you, let him be the first to throw a stone at her.*" (John 8:7) Jesus is not into exposing!

I believe when something of this degree happens, it is best to have someone you can trust, and who has spiritual understanding of Scripture, for a private disclosure of sin. Some may say, "I do not need any human to confess my sins, I have Jesus." My answer would be, "Yes, we all have Jesus, but there is strength and power in accountability."

To give an example; when I was at University, I was in ROTC and part of a cross country terrain run team. I wanted to get up early and run a 3-mile course through the hills of Rowan County, Kentucky. But every morning at 5 am when the alarm went off, I turned off the alarm, and then turned my body over and went back to sleep. The floor was cold and the bed was warm. The weather outside was wet from the rain, while the bed was dry. Need I say more? Another member of our terrain run team lived nearby and we agreed to run together each morning. Now when the alarm went off, I knew he would know I slept in. Having to answer to another human being made a difference.

When confessing sin, we make ourselves accountable to another person who will ask us about our continuing progress over temptation. If it is "just me and Jesus," nobody else will know, and we may not be able to walk in victory.

I once read, "Confession is not bringing into the light something that has been hidden from God. Confession simply means that we are agreeing with God about what He already knows."

Healing for the sick

'Is anyone among you sick? Then he must call for the elders of the church and they are to pray over him, anointing him with oil in the name of the Lord and the prayer offered in faith will restore the one who is sick, and the Lord will raise him up, and if he has committed sins, they will be forgiven him. Therefore, confess your sins to one another, and pray for one another so that you may be healed. The effective prayer of a righteous man can accomplish much.' James 5:14-16

Do you attend a church that believes in praying for the sick? According to Scripture, elders or spiritual leaders of the church have a responsibility to pray for the sick, and with prayer, oil is a symbol of the Holy Spirit. As the oil is applied and prayers are spoken out in faith, the Holy Spirit is there. We must always remember that the Holy Spirit is sovereign and can be trusted to glorify Jesus. The effective prayer of the righteous will invite the Holy Spirit to fulfill the Will of the Lord.

Prayer for the sick is more than for physical healing, it is also for the forgiveness of sins. The result is prayer for the body, soul, and Spirit of the person.

Ordination

'Joshua the son of Nun was filled with the spirit of wisdom, for Moses had laid his hands on him.' Deuteronomy 34:9

Leviticus 8-10 describes a week-long process in which Aaron and his sons were ordained as Priests. The people of Israel had two types of leaders, kings and priests. The priests began their ministry when the Israelites were still at Mt. Sinai in the wilderness, while Saul became the first king around 400 years later. Therefore, the office of spiritual leader is older and I think more important than the office of political leader.

In both situations, the Bible shows us that there is a process of laying on hands, and a ritual ceremony installing someone to the office of priest or king. Our focus here is the Ordination of spiritual leaders.

The role of spiritual leader is important because the priest/pastor has a dual purpose. He represents God to his people and he represents his people to God. Some sanctuaries even have an altar, and the pastor will stand behind the altar, facing the people for part of the worship, as he represents God such as when he is preaching. Then he will stand in front of the altar with his back to the people as he represents them such as when he prays.

It is a sobering and awesome responsibility to be a pastor. The pastor has the spiritual responsibility to lead his people into the presence of Jesus Christ. It is a 24 - 7 opportunity to demonstrate the Lordship of Jesus Christ. The pastor lives in a fish bowl because he is always being seen. He can teach the Bible, provide spiritual direction, furnish pastoral counseling, and be an encouragement to his people.

In such a life, the Holy Spirit must be moving in power, giving direction, mercy, and lots of love. There is a day in the life of an ordained minister in which someone lays on hands and prays, bringing him formally into the ministry. This ceremony, when entered into humbly, seeking the Lord's power, is a sacrament.

Marriage

The wedding ceremony is much more than a party, family reunion (for two families), or an opportunity to show off the latest fashion. It is a sobering function in which two people become one.

'For this reason a man shall leave his father and his mother, and be joined to his wife; and they shall become one flesh.' Genesis 2:24

How can anyone know this person they are preparing to marry will still love them in a year, or 10 years, or 50 years? You do not.

How can anyone prepare for the uncertainties of life as two lives are joined? A marriage begins with a wedding, and the wedding must consist of three persons making a commitment to each other, which will last as long as both bride and groom live.

The third person in the wedding is the Holy Spirit. We must invite the Holy Spirit as the third person into the marriage. The sacrament of marriage can then be the start of a confident lifetime which demonstrates the Lordship of Jesus Christ in this couple to the rest of the world.

When I was a pastor and performed weddings, I would meet with the couple prior to their wedding day, because I know they will be too nervous to hear anything I say on the day of the ceremony, so I want them to hear and to understand the words and the charge I will give to them then.

One such charge is "Having fully considered the vow you are about to make, you declare your allegiance to God and to one another. It is not to be entered into unadvisedly but reverently, discreetly and in the fear of the Lord."

The wedding is perhaps the best sacrament where the invocation of the Holy Spirit to be present, not only in the worship service, but throughout their lives, is best understood. I can often feel the tension of uncertainty during devotion to each other and the Lord, as the couple enter their marriage.

Perhaps the best words to describe this are in a song written by Don Francisco titled, "I Could Never Promise You."

I could never promise you on just my strength alone
That all my life I'd care for you, and love you as my own
I've never known the future, I only see today
Words that last a lifetime would be more than I could say

But the love inside my heart today(tonight) is more than
mine alone
It never changes, it never fails, never seeks it's own
And by the God who gives it, and who lives in me and you
I know the words I speak today(tonight) are words I'm
going to do

And so I stand before you now for all to hear and see
I promise you in Jesus' name the love He's given me
And through the years on earth and as eternity goes by
The life and love He's given us are never going to die.

Like all the other sacraments, the ceremony or ritual can be going through the motions, or it can be a celebration of the presence of the Lord as the participants seek to bring the Holy Spirit into their lives, so they can walk in the power of the Lord for the glory of the Lord.

Let us examine, a few observations about sacraments, as we close out this chapter.

'Now He who establishes us with you in Christ and anointed us is God, who also sealed us and gave us the Spirit in our hearts as a pledge.'

2 Corinthians 1:21-22

'Do not grieve the Holy Spirit of God, by whom you were sealed for the day of redemption.' Ephesians 4:30

Many sacraments involve laying on of hands with prayer. This is done for Ordination, praying for the sick, Confirmation, and often in a wedding as the couple receives prayer for their Marriage. Also, ceremonies such as weddings, Ordination, Baptism, and Confirmation are life events, in which the participants enter a new phase of life. Participating in the sacrament is a call to the Holy Spirit to be present, not only in the observance, but also for the rest of their lives, to bring permanence to the vows and commitments being made.

CHAPTER 18

Obedience

If the Church is going to live victorious, the Church must be a people who represent Jesus Christ in all we do, all we believe and all we say. It is the Lord Jesus Himself, and the Holy Spirit, who are combating the forces of darkness on our behalf. We get involved as we live for Christ, as we take the weapons of warfare, using them correctly, and as we walk in righteousness and obedience.

Obedience is not a term we enjoy. Christians would rather think about the mercy and grace of our Lord, rather than His displeasure when we sin. Nevertheless, our obedience is very important to Jesus. In fact, He requires obedience.

Several years ago, as happens often for many Christians, I was reading my daily Bible study when suddenly a verse jumped off the page at me. In Deuteronomy 10:12, I read, '*What does the Lord your God require from you?*'

I had not given requirement from the Lord much thought. This phrase made me think. We hear a lot about requirements in sermons and Christian teachings. Things like attendance in worship and Sunday school, tithing, good deeds, praying, Bible study, and wearing clean clothes to church, come to my mind. Moses does not list any of these as requirements. But the Lord has different thoughts when it comes to requirements.

'Now, Israel, what does the LORD your God require from you, but to fear the LORD your God, to walk in all His ways and love Him, and to serve the LORD your God with all your heart and with all your soul, and to keep the LORD'S commandments and His statutes which I am commanding you today for your good?' Deuteronomy 10:12-13

A close study of this passage shows twice the Lord speaks of obedience. "Walk in all His ways" and "keep the Lord's commandments" are both exhortations for obedience. Therefore, we must conclude that obedience is important from the Lord's point of view.

But how is obedience a weapon of strategic spiritual warfare? The Lord promised as we obey, He will protect us by being an enemy to our enemies.

'But if you truly obey his voice and do all that I say, then I will be an enemy to your enemies and an adversary to your adversaries.' Exodus 23:22

But also, the Bible teaches that if we compromise with the world's belief systems then we open ourselves to problems. If we drive sin out of our lives and seek Jesus, and His ways only, then we will be blessed. But if we allow the ways of the world to have dominion, then they will create trouble.

'Speak to the sons of Israel and say to them, 'When you cross over the Jordan into the land of Canaan, then you shall drive out all the inhabitants of the land from before you, and destroy all their figured stones, and destroy all their molten images and demolish all their high places; and you shall take possession of the land and live in it, for I have given the land to you to possess it. But if you do not drive out the inhabitants of the land from before you, then it shall come about that those whom you let remain of them will become as pricks in your eyes and as thorns in your sides, and they will trouble you in the land in which you live. And as I plan to do to them, so I will do to you.' Numbers 33:51-56

One example of this would be truth, because a lie never glorifies Jesus. He is truth. I know from personal past failures how easy it is for Christian leaders to lie. We do not think of it as a lie, only a little way to make us look better. This is especially true of statistics, by sending denominational reports which exaggerate average attendance, or the number of salvations at crusades.

Compromising with total truth creates an opening for darkness. The Bible states plainly that the devil is a liar and there is no truth in him.

'You are of your father the devil, and you want to do the desires of your father. He was a murderer from the beginning, and does not stand in the truth because there is no truth in him. Whenever he speaks a lie, he speaks from his own nature, for he is a liar and the father of lies.' John 8:44

As we are truthful, we then open our hearts and lives to the power of the Holy Spirit. There is a freedom in the Truth and bondage in lies. As we walk in Truth and proclaim the Truth both in fact and in Spirit, we generate a power to defeat the lies of the enemy and glorify Jesus Christ.

Continuing our look at Deuteronomy 10:12-13; the first requirement is to fear the Lord. I have not observed the fear of the Lord preached or taught today. In fact, each time I have preached or taught on the fear of the Lord, there is strong vocal opposition. Someone has always come to me claiming that God is love, and we are not supposed to be afraid of Him. In our society, it is obvious there is little fear of the Lord, by the way His commandments are ignored or brushed aside. We do not understand nor appreciate His power and His anger at sin. We have not embraced His desire for obedience, nor the consequences of disobedience. People who walk in the fear of the Lord have a divine protector.

'And we are witnesses of these things; and so is the Holy Spirit, whom God has given to those who obey Him.' Acts 5:32

How does obedience relate to spiritual warfare?

Obedience puts the power in the other weapons we use in strategic spiritual warfare. It is important that we understand the weapons of strategic spiritual warfare are not magic. It is not merely a case of wearing a cross or saying Bible verses aloud to change your situation. The foundation of the spiritual warrior is a right relationship with Jesus Christ. The best Scriptural example is found in Acts 19.

'But also some of the Jewish exorcists who went from place to place, attempted to name over those who had the evil spirit's the Name of the Lord Jesus, saying, 'I adjure you by Jesus whom Paul preaches.' Seven sons of one Sceva were doing this. And the evil spirit answered and said to them, 'I recognize Jesus, and I know about Paul, but who are you?' And the man to whom was the evil spirit, leaped on them and subjected all of them and overpowered them, so that they fled out from that house naked and wounded.' Acts 19:13-16

We are in a dark world and our obedience to our King displays not only to those who know us, but also into the Heavenly realm, that we are now in the Kingdom of His Son. Righteousness binds the power of the darkness and releases the power of the Lord, resulting in Jesus gaining honor and glory through His work in us.

'So that you will walk in a manner worthy of the Lord, to please Him in all respects, bearing fruit in every good work and increasing in the knowledge of God.' Colossians 1.10

'For He rescued us from the domain of darkness, and transferred us to the Kingdom of His beloved Son.' 1 Colossians 1.13

Obedience is not only for individuals but also for groups.

Groups such as congregations, cities, nations, or ministries can be blessed or cursed by spiritual powers, based on whether their leaders and/or polices, follow the principles of Scriptures.

We are the army of the Lord, and as we engage in spiritual battles, we must be diligent to walk in Holiness. It was vital for the Israelites led by Moses and Joshua, and it is equally vital for the Church today.

'When you go out as an army against your enemies, you shall keep yourself from every evil thing.' Deuteronomy 23:9

Not only does obedience invite the Holy Spirit into your life and, but the opposite is also true. Disobedience invites demons into your life. This is especially true for governments, congregations and other organizations. Nations can pass laws against the Nature and Character of Jesus, resulting in demonic activity, because the demons are invited into the nation.

I saw a paper written many years ago, showing various social issue statistics, with a comparison based on the Supreme Court decision to ban prayer in the public schools. Issues such as teen pregnancy, crime, drug use, and divorce skyrocketed after this decision. Looking at the situation through the eyes of the Lord, one cannot help but see the powers of darkness moved into our society with a new freedom because the Supreme Court invited them. This is why it's so critical to pray for government leaders, as Paul wrote to Timothy.

'First of all, then, I urge that entreaties and prayers, petitions and thanksgivings, be made on behalf of all men, for kings and all who are in authority, so that we may lead a tranquil and quiet life in all godliness and dignity.' 1 Timothy 2:1-2

A government in obedience will prosper.

'Now it shall be, if you diligently obey the LORD your God, being careful to do all His commandments which I command you today, the LORD your God will set you high above all the nations of the earth.' Deuteronomy 28:1

Looking at the worldwide economic condition today, how does this truth play a part? One example is 2 Thessalonians 3:6-12, which says,

'*Now we command you, brethren, in the name of our Lord Jesus Christ, that you keep away from every brother who leads an unruly life and not according to the tradition which you received from us. For you yourselves know how you ought to follow our example, because we did not act in an undisciplined manner among you, nor did we eat anyone's bread without paying for it, but with labor and hardship we kept working night and day so that we would not be a burden to any of you; not because we do not have the right to this, but in order to offer ourselves as a model for you, so that you would follow our example. For even when we were with you, we used to give you this order: if anyone is not willing to work, then he is not to eat, either. For we hear that some among you are leading an undisciplined life, doing no work at all, but acting like busybodies. Now such persons we command and exhort in the Lord Jesus Christ to work in quiet fashion and eat their own bread.*'

The welfare system is ruining the economies of the Western world. There is a "get something for nothing" mentality present, which is simply not healthy or Biblical.

In 2012, I worked with the *Boys Brigade* program at Townsend Street Presbyterian Church of the lower Shankill in Belfast, Northern Ireland. The statistics on unemployment, education, literacy, crime, drug abuse, and teen pregnancy show the Shankill with the lowest standard of living in all of Northern Ireland. In my work with the *Boys Brigade*, we asked some of our participants who are around ten years old a question I was asked dozens of times when I was young, "What are you going to do when you grow up?" I answered in many ways depending on my mood, and my latest interest. I wanted to be an astronaut one day, a cowboy the next, a doctor the next, or perhaps even a professional baseball player for the New York Yankees. The specific answer may have changed but what never changed was my expectation of an exciting and interesting adult life.

These boys told us they did not want to do anything when they grew up. By the time, I left Belfast; I had realized it was not that they did not want to do anything when they grew up. Due to "The Troubles" gripping the area, the hope of ever becoming an adult was taken from them. They had watched their families being broken apart, as members were being arrested or shot. What was common to them was uncommon to me. This is where we can be in danger of judging a person, because in truth, we do not know all the facts.

Where hope has been taken from our young people, it is of the utmost importance, when possible, as adults that we do everything we can to provide a good example of character and work standards, and as business creators, to give hope to those who watch us from the side line.

A society filled with workers will be blessed of the Lord. It is a fundamental Biblical principle.

Obedience is a witness to those who are not Christians.

This book is about spiritual warfare and one truth about this war is, Jesus wins! If you do not believe me read the back of the Bible! This is glorious, and should be a great encouragement. But there is a difference in winning the war and daily battles. In daily battles, some can be lost, but in whole, the war will be won!

Our obedience is a key in those battles. How many souls are in hell today because of the horrible actions on the part of some Christian? What we say and how we act is important. We truly are the only Bible some people will ever read. Jesus said, "...*He who has seen Me has seen the Father...*" (John 14:9). In a similar way, many people believe if they have seen you then they have seen Jesus. If we are poor witness by our disobedience, then a battle could be lost.

Part of our strategic spiritual warfare could be during our prayers of repentance, to include a prayer for others to have a memory loss and blindness to the sin of our past. We should ask the Lord to heal the hearts of those we have hurt.

Remember strategic spiritual warfare is the long-term battle. As someone observes your obedience to Jesus, it makes an impression on them.

'In the same way, you wives, be submissive to your own husbands so that even if any them are disobedient to the word, they may be won without a word by the behavior of their wives, as they observe your chaste and respectful behavior. Your adornment must not be merely external but let it be the hidden person of the heart, with the imperishable quality of a gentle and quiet spirit, which is precious in the sight of God.' 1 Peter 3:1-4

This verse encourages good behavior on the part of wives with unsaved husbands, in order to influence their husbands to follow Jesus. But it obviously extends to all of us in our relationships with non-Christians.

It is very sobering to be with members of the persecuted Church. When they share about the arrests, torture, and even the murder of family members for Jesus, it gets very emotional. But then, when they express their determination to live for Jesus, even to the point of facing death, with love for their accusers, it gets really powerful. I have heard Christians say that their prayer is, if they should be killed, their death would be an instrument used by Jesus to win their captors to Christ.

'We overcome him by the blood of the Lamb, and because of the word of our testimony, (act of obedience) and they did not love their life even when faced with death (another act of obedience).' Revelation 12:11

Obedience is based on a personal relationship with Jesus.

There are many well-meaning Christians who struggle with their obedience. They feel Jesus cannot love them nor accept them if they are ever disobedient. We are not obedient to gain salvation, we are obedient because we are saved, and have a desire to honor

Jesus with our behavior. Obedience should never be based on a set of rules, or religious ritual. Obedience is based on a personal relationship with Jesus, and more specifically on the ability within the relationship to hear His voice giving us guidance and encouragement.

The Bible says in many places that we are to obey His voice. This assumes a desire to hear the Lord, and an ability to develop spiritual understanding is necessary to walk in the fullness of obedience. The following are key Scriptures as we are exhorted to hear and obey His voice:

'Now then, if you will indeed obey My voice and keep My covenant, then you shall be My own possession among all the peoples, for all the earth is Mine.' Exodus 19:5

'The people said to Joshua, We will serve the Lord our God and we will obey His voice.' Joshua 24:24

'Why then did you not obey the voice of the Lord, but rushed upon the spoil and did what was evil in the sight of the Lord?' 1 Samuel 15:19

'Because they did not obey the voice of the Lord their God, but transgressed His covenant, even all that Moses the servant of the Lord commanded; they would neither listen nor do it.' 2 Kings 18:12

'But My people did not listen to My voice, and Israel did not obey Me.' Psalm 81:11

'But this is what I commanded them, saying, 'Obey My voice, and I will be your God, and you will be My people; and you will walk in all the way which I command you, that it may be well with you.' Jeremiah 7:23

'You shall say to them, 'This is the nation that did not obey the voice of the Lord their God or accept correction; truth has perished and has been cut off from their mouth.' Jeremiah 7:28

Our obedience will release and loose the character of Jesus

through us. Those traits of truth, purity, love, light and life, will do more to win a person to Jesus than merely casting out demons.

Ultimately it will be the obedience of the Church which will bring the Kingdom of Heaven to the Earth, and bring final victory, and final glory to Jesus Christ.

CHAPTER 19

Fasting

Jesus told us to fast.

'Whenever you fast, do not put on a gloomy face as the hypocrites do, for they neglect their appearance so that they will be noticed by men when they are fasting. Truly I say to you, they have their reward in full. But you, when you fast, anoint your head and wash your face so that your fasting will not be noticed by men, but by your Father who is in secret; and your Father who sees what is done in secret will reward you.' Matthew 6:16-18

Notice Jesus did not say "if" you fast but "when" you fast. Fasting is an expected part of the Christian life. Most Christians do not understand fasting. In fact, I fear very little teaching or preaching is done on fasting, by those in the pulpits of the Western World.

Fasting has always been a vital part in the lives of the leaders of the Kingdom of Heaven. For example, Moses fasted on the Mount of Sinai.

'So he (Moses) was there with the LORD forty days and forty nights; he did not eat bread or drink water. And he wrote on the tablets the words of the covenant, the Ten Commandments.' Exodus 34:28

Elijah fasted prior to his major mission for the Lord.

'The angel of the Lord came again the second time and touched him and said, 'Arise, eat, because the journey is too great for you.' So he (Elijah) arose and ate and drank, and went in the strength of that food forty days and forty nights to Horeb, the mountain of God.' 1 Kings 19:7-8

King David fasted when the son of his adulterous relationship was born very sickly. He wanted to seek the Lord earnestly and sincerely on behalf of his new-born son, in 2 Samuel 12.

v15 '...Then the Lord struck the child that Uriah's widow bore to David, so that he was very sick. David therefore inquired of God for the child; and David fasted and went and lay all night on the ground. The elders of his household stood beside him in order to raise him up from the ground, but he was unwilling and would not eat food with them. Then it happened on the seventh day that the child died. And the servants of David were afraid to tell him that the child was dead, for they said, 'Behold, while the child was still alive, we spoke to him and he did not listen to our voice. How then can we tell him that the child is dead, since he might do himself harm!' But when David saw that his servants were whispering together, David perceived that the child was dead; so David said to his servants, 'Is the child dead?' And they said, 'He is dead.' So David arose from the ground, washed, anointed himself, and changed his clothes; and he came into the house of the LORD AND WORSHIPED. THEN HE CAME TO HIS OWN HOUSE, AND WHEN HE REQUESTED, THEY SET FOOD BEFORE HIM AND HE ATE. Then his servants said to him, 'What is this thing that you have done? While the child was alive, you fasted and wept; but when the child died, you arose and ate food.' He said, 'While the child was still alive, I fasted and wept; for I said, 'Who knows, the LORD MAY BE GRACIOUS TO ME, THAT THE CHILD MAY LIVE.' But now he has died; why should I fast? Can I bring him back again? I will go to him, but he will not return to me.' 2 Samuel 12:15-23

Fasting is a weapon in spiritual warfare when we are seeking the Lord with all of our being. We can demonstrate a sacrificial attitude in petitioning the Lord for a need, or in an attitude of intercession.

In fact, Jesus told his disciples sometimes it takes prayer and fasting to win some spiritual battles. In Matthew 17:14-21, a man brings his demon possessed son to the followers of Jesus. Unfortunately, Jesus is on the Mount of Transfiguration with Peter, James, and John at this point. When Jesus returns, He ministers to the man and his son. Then, when the disciples came to Jesus, privately asking, "Why could we not drive it out?"; Jesus responded by telling them that "this kind does not go out except by prayer and fasting."

There was fasting as a major weapon of spiritual warfare in the days of Esther. (Esther 4:16) Her cousin Mordecai was fasting in sackcloth and ashes. He begged her to do something because she was the queen and should have the ear of the king. But even the queen could not simply enter the presence of the king unless invited. If she appeared without an invitation she could be killed. So, she joined the fast and motivated those in her court to fast also. This group fast resulted in her gaining the ear of the king. Haman the enemy of the Jews was hanged and the Jews were allowed to arm themselves for defense. As a result, the Jewish people won a great victory over the forces who sought their destruction.

Nehemiah fasted to gain power for his return to Jerusalem and restore the Holy City to the Jewish people, who are God's chosen.

'They said to me, 'The remnant there in the province who survived the captivity are in great distress and reproach, and the wall of Jerusalem is broken down and its gates are burned with fire.' When I heard these words, I sat down and wept and mourned for days; and I was fasting and praying before the God of heaven.' Nehemiah 1:3-4

Ezra proclaimed a fast when a group of Hebrews were returning to Jerusalem from Persia, without protection from King Artazerxes,

'Then I proclaimed a fast there at the river of Ahava, that we might humble ourselves before our God to seek from Him safe journey for us, our little ones, and all our possessions.' Ezra 8:21

Many Jewish holidays include fasting such as Feast of booths, (Leviticus 23:34), Yom Kippur, Purim, Passover, and Tzom Tammuz, which is the date that Nebuchadnezzar broke down the walls of Jerusalem and ended the Temple worship. Interestingly, when the Romans attacked Jerusalem in 70 AD and destroyed the Second Temple, it was the same day on the Hebrew Calendar.

The Jewish understanding of fasting for the Temple gives an understanding of strategic spiritual warfare. The Jewish tradition has written that the fast for the Temple is to seek empowerment, to create favor with God, so that the sin which caused the Temple destruction would be removed, and the exile without the Temple would end.

Of course, Jesus fasted, and He is our supreme example. After His Baptism, Jesus was led up by the Spirit into the wilderness. The Bible tells us, after He had fasted for forty days and forty nights; He became hungry and was tempted by the devil. But did you realize Jesus fasted at other times as well? In John 4:7-30, Jesus is speaking with the woman at the well while the disciples have gone into the city to buy food. During the conversation, the disciples return and in verse John 4:31, urge Jesus to eat. But Jesus replied that He has food to eat that they do not know about. They responded by asking each other who brought Jesus something to eat? At this point, Jesus tells them that His food is to "do the will of Him who sent Me and to accomplish His work."

This implies to me that Jesus is fasting. After all, one of the temptations He faced in the wilderness was to turn stones into bread. His response was, *'Man does not live by bread alone but on every Word which proceeds out of the mouth of God.'* Matthew 4:4

Jesus was enjoying spiritual food and refreshment in John 4.

Fasting was prominent in the early Church, as described to us in the Book of Acts. Fasting can help each Christian be more spiritually aware. Hearing the voice of the Lord is enhanced by fasting. One of the most exciting Scriptures to me, is found in Acts.

'Now there were at Antioch, in the church that was there, prophets and teachers: Barnabas, and Simeon who was called Niger, and Lucius of Cyrene, and Manaen who had been brought up with Herod the tetrarch, and Saul. While they were ministering to the Lord and fasting, the Holy Spirit said, 'Set apart for Me Barnabas and Saul for the work to which I have called them.' Then when they had fasted and prayed and laid their hands on them, they sent them away.' Acts 13:1-3

We often hear about ministering to one another but this group was ministering to the Lord and they were fasting. They were listening for direction from Jesus. And Jesus spoke! The result of this prayer and fasting session was the first missionary journey of Paul (known as Saul in this passage).

Fasting, is getting serious about hearing from the Lord. When a Christian is serious about hearing from the Lord, and determined to do as he is directed, he has been equipped with great weapons to conduct spiritual warfare.

Fasting can be done by individuals and groups. Jesus said, when we fast we are not to be like those religious people of His day who wore pale makeup, dressed in rags, had long faces, and otherwise let everyone know they were fasting and suffering for the Lord. Jesus told us to keep our fast secret. We should look our best, with make up on our faces. We are to put on our best clothes and act joyful. Above all, do not let it be known we are fasting. But of course, if we are fasting as a group, then the others in the group will know.

Keeping our fasts secret is not really a problem, we can see from Scripture that there are many times when groups were fasting together. The group even reached out to encourage others to join them in the fast. It seems that the Spirit of what Jesus is teaching can still apply. We are not to be sad. We are not to be fasting in order to be seen by man. We are not to be fasting as a way of showing we are somehow better, or more spiritual, than those around us.

A group fast can actually have many advantages. While true, we are in the presence of the Lord at all times, there are moments when a real live human being can help us do what is necessary when we are tempted to quit. Just like when I was on the terrain run team in college, which I explained above. To have another person for accountability has many advantages.

When it comes to fasting, I would often sense a leading to fast, and then was invited to a great place to eat for lunch. So, I make a deal with the Lord to fast "tomorrow," and "tomorrow" never comes, so I miss the blessing of the fast. However, when a group has a need and we agree to take it to the Lord in prayer with fasting, I have the power to stay on my fast.

Fasting can be many different types of sacrifice. Going without food is the most common, but if a decision is made to spend the night in prayer, then sleep is being denied. Other types of fasting can be fasting from television, movies, driving a car, sports, ice cream, or even Christian fellowship, as strange as that may seem.

Fasting is spiritual warfare.

Strategic spiritual weapons such as the act of fasting are only part of the bigger picture. First, it is not just the fasting but it is the prayer, while fasting. It is the surrender to the Lord's will to fast. It is the sacrifice of rejecting a basic human need for a short period of time, to gain spiritual benefit. As we fast, it gives the Holy Spirit an opportunity to draw us closer to the Lord, and to His will for our lives. As we fast, we develop self-discipline. Derek Prince used to say that he told his body when to eat, and would not allow his body to tell him when to eat.

Many of the giants of Church history, especially in the Pentecostal movement, have gone into isolation, such as in the loft of a barn, and stayed there fasting until they "broke through" to the Lord. These were life changing experiences, which many do not experience today because we are too busy with our daily lives to take time to seriously seek the Lord. In a way, fasting is declaring to the Lord and to the powers of darkness that we are serious about our Christian walk. We are serious about our prayer. We are serious about seeking the Lord's answer to our prayers and concerns. As we fast and as the Holy Spirit is energized by our fasting, the power of the Lord is manifested more completely in our lives.

Many spiritual truths must be experienced because there simply are no words to describe it. Fasting is one of those experiences and you should try it!

CHAPTER 20

Gospel Music

Music is a huge part of every person's life, as we go into shops, watch TV, listen to the radio… It seems only a few minutes will go past without hearing music in our life nowadays.

Music is played in the background of every television drama and movie, changing our mood of what we see, to what we hear. We know then, something is about to happen!

Once when I was a chaplain with a large hospital in Florida, my supervisor shared with me an experience that he had with the power of Gospel Music. He was also a pastor in addition to being a chaplain and a troubled man came to his worship service. The man began to react violently when the choir sang the special music, which was especially lively and powerful. As people began to minister deliverance, my chaplain friend became aware that it was the power of the Gospel music, which the Lord used to bring cleansing from the demons, which inhabited this man.

The man gave his life to Jesus, and then told his story. In his younger days, he was obsessed with music. He would especially seek out the hard rock and rap songs which would depict violence and perversion. He dabbled in the occult, which also included harsh music. As the Gospel music filled the room, the demonic powers reacted to the message of Jesus Christ. Christian music can therefore be a powerful weapon that we can use to bring victory in our spiritual life.

Music is a creation from the Lord and a gift to man. Music is mentioned in every section of the Bible. Even before the flood, Jubal was the father of all who played musical instruments.

'His brother's name was Jubal; he was the father of all those who play the lyre and pipe.' Genesis 4:21

When Pharaoh and his army were drowned in the Red Sea, the Israelites celebrated with singing.

'Then Moses and the sons of Israel sang this song to the LORD, and said, 'I will sing to the LORD, for He is highly exalted; The horse and its rider He has hurled into the sea.' Exodus 15:1

David was hired to play his harp when an evil spirit terrorized King Saul. Music provided the power which would force the evil spirit away, especially when played by a man after God's own heart.

'Now the Spirit of the LORD departed from Saul, and an evil spirit from the LORD terrorized him. Saul's servants then said to him, 'Behold now, an evil spirit from God is terrorizing you. Let our lord now command your servants who are before you. Let them seek a man who is a skillful player on the harp; and it shall come about when the evil spirit from God is on you, that he shall play the harp with his hand, and you will be well.' So Saul said to his servants, 'Provide for me now a man who can play well and bring him to me.' Then one of the young men said, 'Behold, I have seen a son of Jesse the Bethlehemite who is a skillful musician, a mighty man of valor, a warrior, one prudent in speech, and a handsome man; and the LORD is with him.' So Saul sent messengers to Jesse and said, 'Send me your son David who is with the flock.' Then David came to Saul and attended him; and Saul loved him greatly, and he became his armor bearer. So it came about whenever the evil spirit from God came to Saul, David would take the harp and play it with his hand; and Saul would be refreshed and be well, and the evil spirit would depart from him. 1 Samuel 16:14-23

When David became the King, he appointed musicians for the tabernacle.

'Now these are those whom David appointed over the service of song in the house of the LORD, after the ark rested there. They ministered with song before the tabernacle of the tent of meeting, until Solomon had built the house of the LORD in Jerusalem; and they served in their office according to their order.' 1 Chronicles 6:31-32

When the Ark of the Covenant was brought into Jerusalem, King David, himself, led the worship through the streets with music, dancing, and celebration. He got so involved in the worship his wife was embarrassed. King David must have wanted to please the Lord more than he wanted to please the people around him.

'Now David was clothed with a robe of fine linen with all the Levites who were carrying the ark, and the singers and Chenaniah the leader of the singing with the singers. David also wore an ephod of linen. Thus all Israel brought up the ark of the covenant of the LORD with shouting, and with sound of the horn, with trumpets, with loud-sounding cymbals, with harps and lyres. It happened when the ark of the covenant of the LORD came to the city of David, that Michal the daughter of Saul looked out of the window and saw King David leaping and celebrating; and she despised him in her heart.' 1 Chronicles 15:27-29

When Jehoshaphat was King of Judah, he faced war, yet chooses to put those who sang praises to the Lord in front of his Army. The Lord gave them a great victory without "firing a shot."

'Now it came about after this that the sons of Moab and the sons of Ammon, together with some of the Meunites, came to make war against Jehoshaphat. Jehoshaphat was afraid and turned his attention to seek the LORD, and proclaimed a fast throughout all Judah. So Judah gathered together to seek help from the LORD; they even came from all the cities of Judah to seek the LORD. Then in the midst of the assembly the Spirit of the LORD came upon Jahaziel the son of Zechariah, the son of Benaiah, the son of Jeiel, the son of

Mattaniah, the Levite of the sons of Asaph; and he said, 'Listen, all Judah and the inhabitants of Jerusalem and King Jehoshaphat: thus says the LORD to you, 'Do not fear or be dismayed because of this great multitude, for the battle is not yours but God's.' You need not fight in this battle; station yourselves, stand and see the salvation of the LORD on your behalf, O Judah and Jerusalem. Do not fear or be dismayed; tomorrow go out to face them, for the LORD is with you.' They rose early in the morning and went out to the wilderness of Tekoa; and when they went out, Jehoshaphat stood and said, 'Listen to me, O Judah and inhabitants of Jerusalem, put your trust in the LORD your God and you will be established. Put your trust in His prophets and succeed.' When he had consulted with the people, he appointed those who sang to the LORD and those who praised Him in holy attire, as they went out before the army and said, 'Give thanks to the LORD, for His lovingkindness is everlasting.' When they began singing and praising, the LORD set ambushes against the sons of Ammon, Moab and Mount Seir, who had come against Judah; so they were routed.' 2 Chronicles 20:1-22

In the Psalms, we see a constant flow of praise to the Lord through song and music.

'The LORD is my strength and my shield; My heart trusts in Him, and I am helped; Therefore my heart exults, and with my song I shall thank Him.' Psalm 28:7

'Sing for joy in the LORD, O you righteous ones; Praise is becoming to the upright. Give thanks to the LORD with the lyre; Sing praises to Him with a harp of ten strings. Sing to Him a new song; Play skillfully with a shout of joy.' Psalm 33:1-3

'The LORD will command His lovingkindness in the daytime; And His song will be with me in the night, A prayer to the God of my life.' Psalm 42:8

Notice what you just read there in Psalm 42? David writes *'His song will be with me.'* We will come back to this thought later.

'I will also praise You with a harp, Even Your truth, O my God; To You I will sing praises with the lyre, O Holy One of Israel.' Psalm 71:22

'O sing to the LORD a new song, For He has done wonderful things, His right hand and His holy arm have gained the victory for Him.' Psalm 98:1

'Shout joyfully to the LORD, all the earth. Serve the LORD with gladness; Come before Him with joyful singing.' Psalm 100:1-2

'Sing to the LORD a new song, And His praise in the congregation of the godly ones. Let Israel be glad in his Maker; Let the sons of Zion rejoice in their King. Let them praise His name with dancing; Let them sing praises to Him with timbrel and lyre.' Psalm 149:1-3

'Praise the LORD! Praise God in His sanctuary; Praise Him in His mighty expanse. Praise Him for His mighty deeds; Praise Him according to His excellent greatness. Praise Him with trumpet sound; Praise Him with harp and lyre. Praise Him with timbrel and dancing; Praise Him with stringed instruments and pipe. Praise Him with loud cymbals; Praise Him with resounding cymbals. Let everything that has breath praise the LORD. Praise the LORD!' Psalm 150

There are songs of praise to the Lord and there are songs of fools. Needless to say, we need to discern and embrace the songs of praise. The songs of fools will result in exile.

'It is better to listen to the rebuke of a wise man. Than for one to listen to the song of fools.' Ecclesiastes 7:5

'Woe to those who rise early in the morning that they may pursue strong drink, Who stay up late in the evening that wine may inflame them! Their banquets are accompanied by lyre and harp, by tambourine and flute, and by wine; But they do not pay attention to the deeds of the LORD, Nor do they consider the work of His hands. Therefore My people go into exile for their lack of knowledge; And their honorable men are famished, And their multitude is parched with thirst.' Isaiah 5:11-13

In the days of Nebuchadnezzar in Babylon, there was a call to worship with many musical instruments. But this worship of course was to honor Nebuchadnezzar rather than the Lord.

'Then Nebuchadnezzar the king sent word to assemble the satraps, the prefects and the governors, the counselors, the treasurers, the judges, the magistrates and all the rulers of the provinces to come to the dedication of the image that Nebuchadnezzar the king had set up. Then the herald loudly proclaimed: 'To you the command is given, O peoples, nations and men of every language, that at the moment you hear the sound of the horn, flute, lyre, trigon, psaltery, bagpipe and all kinds of music, you are to fall down and worship the golden image that Nebuchadnezzar the king has set up. But whoever does not fall down and worship shall immediately be cast into the midst of a furnace of blazing fire.' Daniel 3:2-6

After Shadrach, Meshach, and Abednego refused to bow and survived the fiery furnace, Nebuchadnezzar declared the God of Shadrach, Meshach, and Abednego, as the one true God.

One of the best examples of how music is a weapon in spiritual warfare is seen in Acts 16. Paul and Silas are in the Philippian jail, praying and singing praises. This made such an impression on the jailer after the earthquake; he wanted to know how he could be saved.

'The crowd rose up together against them, and the chief magistrates tore their robes off them and proceeded to order them to be beaten with rods. When they had struck them with many blows, they threw them into prison, commanding the jailer to guard them securely; and he, having received such a command, threw them into the inner prison and fastened their feet in the stocks. But about midnight Paul and Silas were praying and singing hymns of praise to God, and the prisoners were listening to them; and suddenly there came a great earthquake, so that the foundations of the prison house were shaken; and immediately all the doors were opened and everyone's chains were unfastened. When the jailer awoke and saw the prison doors opened, he drew his sword and was about to kill himself, supposing

that the prisoners had escaped. But Paul cried out with a loud voice, saying, 'Do not harm yourself, for we are all here!' And he called for lights and rushed in, and trembling with fear he fell down before Paul and Silas, and after he brought them out, he said, 'Sirs, what must I do to be saved?' They said, 'Believe in the Lord Jesus, and you will be saved, you and your household.' Acts 16:22-30

The apostle Paul wrote to the Colossians that we are to use music for the purpose of thanksgiving, and to provide encouragement to other Christians.

'Let the word of Christ richly dwell within you, with all wisdom teaching and admonishing one another with psalms and hymns and spiritual songs, singing with thankfulness in your hearts to God.' Colossians 3:16

Music as Spiritual Warfare

Music is spiritual. Christian music under God will bring the Holy Spirit. Note I wrote – "under God." There is a lot of music out there which I am quite sure would not be acceptable in Heaven, but because someone has placed "Christian" on it, we accept it. This is why; "Discernment of Spirits," which I shared earlier, is so important in our life.

In Psalm 22:3, '...*O You who are holy, O You who are enthroned upon the praises of Israel.'*

It is important at every chance to have praise going up onto our God. The sadness is that even when churches are being built, they have worldly workers playing and singing onto worldly songs, drawing evil in, when in fact, a standard of holiness would not allow this to happen. If the singing or music is not Godly, then it should not be allowed to be played or sung in our churches, homes or cars etc. Why allow a worldly influence when you could influence a listener to the things of God?

David writes in Psalm 42:8, *'His song will be with me.'* It is possible to have the Lord's song in your heart, and sing it under God. Even during deliverance ministry, singing or music can be used to help cause unease with a demon.

David makes a statement that he wants "His song" to be the tune in his head and in his heart. I enjoy praising the Lord with a lively Christian song in my mind. But, sometimes I will go into a store (and it seems music is always playing in stores) and when I leave a different song is playing in my mind. What took place? My mind had taken a seed of a song and was trying to plant it. That's how powerful words and music are!

The Purpose of Music

Martin Luther said, "Next to the Word of God, the noble art of music is the greatest treasure in the world."

The purpose of music is to praise the Lord. Music is to honor the creator not the creation. Music is a gift to us from our Heavenly Father. While not all "secular" music is evil, it is second best. Some "secular" music can have a positive tune and message honoring the goodness in the world. There is a lot of good music. Chris Christian sang a song back in the 1970's, "Why Should the devil Have All the Good Music." It was a song encouraging Christians to sing new songs to honor Jesus.

Music surrounds us and experts can show how certain music can make people feel better or worse. Retailers research shows that people will buy more or less depending on the song/music that is being played in the background. The tracks are played to cause the buyer to slow down and enjoy the shopping experience – you would wonder why that is? For you to purchase more! Next time you're in the dentist, note the music! It's not "rock and roll," or "heavy metal", it is soft and soothing! That's the power of a track!

When we understand the power of song we can see then how it can be such a powerful weapon in spiritual warfare.

CHAPTER 21

Herrnhut

In May 2010, I traveled from Denmark into Germany via train. The train took almost 24 hours from the Northern border with Denmark to the South-eastern border with Poland and the Czech Republic. After three days, I had arrived in a small village of 2,000 people called, Herrnhut. I had never heard of Herrnhut, but this little village is the home of the most important attack against the forces of darkness in the history of the Christian Church. The Kingdom of Heaven is still benefiting from the strategic spiritual warfare conducted in this village over 200 years ago.

In the little village of Berthelsdorf, there was a man of wealth and position. He was educated in Wittenberg, the home of Martin Luther. He was also a devout Christian, willing to give everything he had to advance the cause of Christ. Count Nikolas Ludwig Von Zinzendorf learned of the persecution of the Moravians in nearby Bohemia, which is today the area of Prague, Czech Republic. In fact, John Huss, one of their early leaders, was publicly burned at the stake for heresy in July 1415. This group of believers needed a place of refuge.

In 1722, at the age of 22, Zinzendorf brought them to Saxony and helped them build their new home. Outside the city of Herrnhut today, there is a monument which marks the spot where the first tree was felled to build the city of Herrnhut, which means "Under the care of the Lord" or "Under the Lord's watch." The 300 Moravians who first settled in Herrnhut lived in relative peace, although Count Zinzendorf experienced his share of misunderstanding, persecution, and heartache.

The Moravians were a people of prayer. They would seek the Lord earnestly for opportunities to serve Him. They were also great people of praise. In August 1727, a small group met for prayer, which was a normal event in the life of their community. But this time things were different. The community was experiencing some problems and they wanted to take it to the Lord with a time of intense supplication. There were 48 people, 24 men and 24 women who agreed to spend one hour a day in prayer. They were organized so two people would always be in prayer. This meant twenty-four hours a day and seven days a week. Others soon joined the prayer time.

As the prayer continued so did the presence of the Holy Spirit. The prayer meeting continued all day and into the night. Others were drawn into the praise. Those who left did so reluctantly, and after sleeping, returned. This intense time of prayer continued for the whole week and continued into the next month. This prayer vigil continued 24 hours a day, 7 days a week, for over 110 years!!!

This was not a little, "bless me Lord" prayer time. As the prayers continued through the years, the people were being spiritually prepared for service. They were being filled in an unbelievable way with the power and purpose of the Holy Spirit. Four years into the prayer vigil, Zinzendorf visited Copenhagen, Denmark, in hopes of helping the Lutheran churches there. He encountered a slave who had escaped from St. Thomas, Virgin Islands in the Caribbean. Zinzendorf's heart was touched when hearing about the slavery, and how they suffered. He also knew they needed Jesus. The slave warned Zinzendorf that the slaves worked constantly under the cruel hand of the slave masters. The only way to preach to the slaves would be for the missionaries to become slaves!

Zinzendorf returned to Herrnhut, and the group sought the Lord. One year later, two men felt the Lord wanted them to go. They traveled by foot across Germany and went to St. Thomas, where they established a congregation who were later visited by Count Zinzendorf himself, with many others from Herrnhut who were called to the remain.

When the Lord began to speak, the saints in Herrnhut were ready to listen and obey. The Lord led them to go out into the entire world. In fact, this little community sent over 300 missionaries out to tell the world about Jesus during the time of the prayer vigil. That is equal to the entire population of Herrnhut in 1722.

The Kingdom of Heaven is built on the foundation and work of previous generations. Much of the Kingdom as we know it today has been built on the foundation of Herrnhut. Perhaps one of their most famous adventures happened in 1735, when a group of Moravians from Herrnhut were sent to the British colony of Georgia, in the New World. The ship was small and the seas got rough. There was a genuine panic and fear that the ship could not prevail in the storm. In the midst of the panic, those Moravians choose to worship the Lord Jesus. As others were crying out for Jesus to save them, the Moravians were joyful. The others were in panic, the Moravians were at peace.

There was a young missionary from London who was on his way to preach the Gospel in the new world, who was observing like the others. He also felt the panic and fear of death at sea. He never forgot the joy and peace those Moravians had, and he knew they had something he did not have. He desperately wanted it. His time in Georgia frankly could only be considered a failure. He simply did not have what it took to be a missionary. He kept searching for the answer to the emptiness of his life. After his time was completed in the New World, he returned to London and continued to seek the answer for the nagging doubts he had about life.

Then one day as he was listening to a lecture on the introduction of Luther's commentary on the letter to the Roman's, he felt his heart "strangely warmed." He remembered his conversation with Peter Bohler, of Herrnhut, while on his journey to Georgia. Peter was teaching that salvation could not be earned. It was by grace one is saved. It was faith, which comes not from works on the part of the person, but from the Lord who grants the joy and peace he saw in the lives of those Moravians.

That missionary's name was John Wesley. Because of the 110 year prayer vigil back in Herrnhut, Saxony; one of the greatest evangelists of the Eighteenth Century found salvation through faith in Jesus, by grace. Today, many denominations trace their roots back to John Wesley. Millions of people have found Christ through the Methodists, Wesleyans, Nazarene, Salvation Army, Holiness and Pentecostal denominations. In fact, there is a lot of evidence that much of the Charismatic movement which began in the 1970's trace their spiritual Heritage to John Wesley, and John Wesley's spiritual Heritage can be traced to the Moravians of Herrnhut. Wesley, himself, traveled to Herrnhut many times to observe the ways of the Moravians. His first visit was in 1738, which was soon after his conversion to Christ. Wesley knew how critical the contributions of the Moravians were to the Kingdom of Heaven.

William Carey, considered by many to be the father of modern missions, actually followed the Moravian missionaries. After reading a Moravian missionary journal, Carey exclaimed,

"See what these Moravians have done! Can't we Baptists attempt something in fealty to the same Lord?"[3]

Today, even after being under the spiritual darkness of Adolph Hitler's Nazi's from 1932 to 1945, and under the equally brutal control of atheistic communism from 1945 to 1991, Herrnhut continues to experience a gentile presence of Jesus. I felt it when I came into the village. There was simply a sweet peaceful Spirit which is not present in any other place in the world where I have travelled. Also, there are many Christian symbols along the many

---

3   Rev Hollis Reed, From the Hand of God in History,

         (Philadelphia: John E Potter and Co., 1870)

trails which wind through the countryside. One particular spot has about 20 figures which are all in prayer. The figures are only heads and arms but are all different. It is a message declaring that Herrnhut is a place of prayer.

The results from the 110 year non-stop prayer vigil can be seen all over the world today. When pondering history and the great cities of the world, while New York, London, Jerusalem, Paris, Rome, and dozens of other major cities have influenced the world; perhaps the tiny village of Herrnhut is the one who heads the list in Heaven.

If the world is going to experience a spiritual Awakening it must be the result of fervent, committed, diligent prayer. We do not need to copy the exact form of prayer which took place in Herrnhut, but we need the same Spirit to achieve at least the same results, if not greater.

CHAPTER 22

Ways to Exercise

There are many activities local churches can do in order to participate in strategic spiritual warfare.

Prayer vigils
Prayer walks
Proclaiming in and around your city
C U @ the Cross (See You at the Cross)
40 days of fasting
Bible Reading marathon

As I now move into a section to describe practical ways for a local church to conduct strategic spiritual warfare, I will be giving some rather detailed explanations about how various programs have been conducted, please seek the Lord as to how He wants you to proceed to gain the maximum benefit. I think of a chocolate cake. There are many ways to make a chocolate cake. You can go to the grocery store and buy a chocolate cake mix. There are directions on the box. You can follow those directions and you will end up with a chocolate cake. You can also consult a cookbook, or look up chocolate cake on the internet, for a recipe. If you follow the recipe, you will have a chocolate cake. Of course, you could be like my grandmother, who goes to the cupboard and takes all the necessary ingredients. She will take a dab of this and a pinch of that. At the end of all her work, she has made a chocolate cake from scratch. The point I am making is that there are many ways to make a chocolate cake. Of course, my grandmother's was the best of all. But, all these different ways resulted with a chocolate cake. The same is true for each of the following "programs". Please hear me; I am not saying that you have to do it this way to have success in conducting strategic spiritual warfare. Seek the Lord and follow His way.

It is also important to remember strategic spiritual warfare can be fun. It should be fun to be a Christian. It should be fun to do Christian things. Being with Christians should be more fun than being with those who do not love Jesus. As congregations get involved in the various programs and projects discussed below, I pray you will use this to fellowship together. Christians should joyfully proclaim Jesus and claim His victory.

Prayer Vigils

A congregation who wants to see something really special in the spiritual lives of the members should have a 24-hour prayer vigil. It is simple to organize and pays rich benefits in the life of the congregation. A smaller congregation may want to have a 12-hour prayer vigil which lasts from 9am to 9pm.

I first heard of a congregational prayer vigil in Vicksburg, Mississippi. The First Christian Church conducted an annual prayer vigil the weekend prior to Easter. It began on Friday at noon and concluded Saturday at noon. The following Sunday was Palm Sunday. Promotion for the prayer vigil began about a month prior to the weekend. Usually, the Elders were the leaders and did the organizing.

There was a sign-up sheet, structured in 30 minute blocks.

Members were asked to sign up for a block. Some members wanted to participate more and several signed up for two blocks and prayed for an hour. As the pastor, I would visit those I knew would benefit from the experience, in order to explain the purpose and share the importance. A fact of congregational life is that many members will not participate unless given a personal invitation and urged to be there.

We conducted our prayer vigil in the sanctuary. We placed a comfortable easy chair, a lamp, and a small table in the front. Sometimes there were soft instrumental hymns playing in the background on a tape or CD player. On the table were various devotional books, Bibles and a notebook. Participants could read the Bible or devotion during their time. Many brought their own Bibles of course. The notebook was used as a prayer diary. Each participant was encouraged to write down any thoughts that they might have during their prayer time. It might be a prayer request for others participating to know about. It might be an encouraging thought about the powerful feeling of the moment. This notebook also contained a list of prayer needs, which each participant was urged to pray for, and that they could also add to the list.

As the pastor, I made it my priority to be there for the entire marathon. A group of us would have prayer in the sanctuary at noon as the marathon began. Everyone, except the one praying, then left. I also was there to pray at noon on Saturday as the marathon ended.

On an administrative note, we also asked the elders of the congregation to be present in order to greet participants before and after their time in prayer. They also provided security. I think it is important for the person in prayer to know that they are not alone in the building, especially in the middle of the night. Some congregations have elders sign up for three hour blocks to provide security and a presence.

The following Sunday, there was a time provided in the worship service for those who participated to share what the prayer vigil meant to them.

Prayer Walks

In Guthrie, Kentucky; once a local congregation invited all Christians from all faiths to participate in a Prayer walk for our town. We met in the fellowship hall of the sponsoring congregation at 7AM on Saturday morning. We were then divided into four groups. They tried to have someone from each congregation participating in each of the four groups. The groups then all walked to City Hall (or it could be a town square or courthouse) for a special prayer for Guthrie.

Then each group went its separate way, as designed by the organizing congregation. There were four points of interest in the town. They were the northern most point, southern most point, eastern most point, and western most point. As each group walked to their official prayer point, we would not be just chatting about football, the weather, or something going on at the local school; we would be aware that our town needs prayer and we would be praying for the town. We would pray for the families represented in the homes we are walking past. Each group was led by a member of the sponsoring congregation and they had prepared special places to stop for prayer, such as the post office, school, monument, church buildings, housing projects, day cares, etc. in order to ask the Lord's blessing and direction in an appropriate way.

Then at a given, predetermined time, each group would be in place on the north, south, east, or west side of town. Then for 15 minutes we would face the middle of the town and pray aloud.

Can you picture the view from Heaven? Here are four groups of Christians representing several denominations, circling the town and praying for the town. We were surrounding the town with prayer.

After this we continued in an attitude of prayer as we slowly walked back to the sponsoring church, for a time of sharing and of course, a wonderful breakfast prepared while we were away. The breakfast was especially appreciated as we conducted this prayer walk in November, when it was a very cold day.

In our case, this was a community project sponsored by one congregation. One congregation could do this as well, but I felt the unity projected and added to the power of our prayers. We had people from all denominations, old, young, men, women, teenagers, Blacks and Whites all praying together.

Proclaiming in and Around Your City

Another similar project to a prayer walk around town, is what I call, a proclaiming walk.

First, during this prayer walk, the participants maintain a time of silence and listening for the Lord to speak. The group leader explains the group will stop at a certain point in order to stop and share. There would be several stopping points along the way. The stopping points could be schools, day cares, nursing homes etc. In order to have special prayers for those needs in our society.

Then there would be a time of proclaiming. This requires some advance preparation on the part of those willing to participate. A look at the section on proclaiming the Word is advised to understand the purpose and procedure involved. Special Bible verses and promises would be selected. At various points as appropriate, those Scriptures would be read aloud as prayers to your city.

A simple example but still powerful is to proclaim John 3:16.

'For God so loved (your city) He gave His only begotten Son so that whoever in (this city) would believe in Him, would not perish but have everlasting life.'

Then everyone should pray for the Holy Spirit to sweep through their city and draw people to Him. Ask the Lord to prepare hearts for receiving the Good News. Pray for those under conviction and needing to get saved.

The advance preparation, and this can be a lot of fun and very inspirational, is too look through the Bible and find promises. Take those promises and claim them for your city.

C U @ the Cross (See you at the Cross)

Pastor Jack McKee pastors a dynamic and growing congregation in the Shankill area of Belfast, Northern Ireland. They bought a warehouse on the peace line a few years ago. Prior to the opening of his new facility, Jack stood on the peace line for 40 days between noon and 3 pm each day.

The concept is simple. Make a Cross and then paint "John 3:16" on the Cross. Then pick a spot in public, which could simply be at the front door of your church building.

Again, there are many options and you should be creative on your approach. It could be as simple as one person standing quietly on the doorsteps holding the Cross for an hour a day. It could be several people, with one person holding the Cross while the others pray aloud or silently. It could be a group holding the Cross on the doorsteps, while another group is talking to people as they walk or drive past. They could be passing out tracks and/or witnessing to them. Also, if your event goes for many days, you could have some refreshments (snacks and drinks) to give away to those who stop by. After having "C U @ the Cross" for over a week, there is almost a party atmosphere as people stop by. There is nothing wrong with having praise and displaying the joy of the Lord. It could be one day leading up to a big event or could be for a week or a month or 40 days.[4]

I think it is very important for there to be as many men as possible involved. In my experience, too many men let the women get involved in the spiritual side of Christianity. The spiritual temperature of the Church is directly parallel to the spiritual temperature of the men leading the congregation.

---

4   NOTE: More of Pastor's McKee's story can be read in his book, 'What does it take?' published by Maurice Wylie Media

C U @ The Cross sounds simple but what is the point?

There are several benefits.

1. It would bring attention to your congregation. People would be talking about the people "up there" or "down there" holding the cross.

2. It would bring people of your congregation together. They would be in prayer during the event. They would take turns holding the cross. They would feel good about the work of your local congregation and be a part of making your congregation known to the neighborhood. Too many church buildings are locked up and are inaccessible during the week, while yours would be open and inviting.

3. As you think of strategic spiritual warfare, standing with the cross sends a statement into the Heavenly realm that Jesus is Lord. Standing with the cross is making a public pronouncement that you are a follower of Jesus Christ. You are not ashamed of the Gospel.

4. Several congregations could cooperate and have this event in a neutral public place, which would allow the cross to be seen by as many people as possible.

5. It is important to have information or tracts about your congregation or the Christian life, to give out. Those inquiring can also be invited to join your group and help hold the cross.

6. With the big "John 3:16" on the cross, be prepared for someone to ask what it means. This may surprise you, but it is true. Christian people take a lot of things for granted, but in our society there are an increasing number of people who have never been inside a church building, and who have no knowledge of anything Christian. Instead of reacting in shock, smile and tell them how glad you are they asked.

What does JOHN 3:16 mean? In answering this, it should be stated JOHN is one of the books in the Bible, and 3:16 is a chapter and a verse in John. Each person should be able to quote the verse and explain it as they go along, as follows: "JOHN 3:16 states that God so loved the world (which means the world and everyone in it), He gave His only Son (His only son is Jesus who died on the cross for our sins) and whoever believes in Him (and that means whoever! No matter how bad they are or how good they think they are; no matter what color their skin, or what their political allegiance is; this means whoever believes in Him, whoever believes in Jesus), will not perish, but will have eternal life. And not only will they have eternal life, but they will have the best in life."

Another question you will be asked is, "Why are you doing this?" Answer: Because there is much which divides people in our world, whether it is politics, color, or even religious traditions, and there is much division between us and Jesus, especially our sin. The reason we are doing this is because we want to show the following three things:

1. The cross is the one thing which unites us with each other, and also with God.

2. The cross is not about religious tradition, but is about a relationship with God through Jesus Christ, God's Son, who died on the cross for all of us, and for all of our sins.

3. The cross represents a better way than religious tradition, and a better solution to life's problems, and the better way is Jesus who said, *'I am the way, and the truth and the life; no one comes to the Father, but through Me.'* (John 14:6) We want to introduce you to this same Jesus; not to religious tradition, not even to a congregation, or denomination, but to Jesus.

40 Days of Fasting

Fasting is taught in many places of Scripture. The concept of fasting for 40 days was practiced by Moses, Elijah and Jesus. It is the ultimate fast. A congregation can fast for 40 days as well. It is a simple concept. During the 40 days, there is always someone in the congregation who is praying and fasting.

The organization is quite simple. A sign-up sheet is maintained with a calendar listing the 40 days. There is room on each day for someone's name to go on either breakfast, lunch, or supper.

The rules are quite simple. If someone has signed up to fast for breakfast, then after the previous evening meal, they do not eat until the lunch meal around noon. The person signed up for lunch may have breakfast but will not eat again until the evening meal around 5PM. The person signed up for supper can have lunch by 1PM and then not eat again until breakfast the next morning.

Each participant is asked to spend the time normally eating in prayer. As with the prayer vigil, there could be a notebook with prayer needs provided. But the 40 days of prayer and fasting does not lend itself to one place. Many participants will fast at home for breakfast and would fast at work for lunch; therefore, it is difficult to have a notebook for thoughts and inspirational notations, which would be passed from one participant to the next. However, it is good to have several meetings each week in which participants are urged to attend, to share, and have a group prayer.

As the 40 days progress, there may be some members of the congregation who did not want to participate at first, but after hearing the experiences of others, or after having re-evaluated the opportunity, they are ready to become involved. There are two ways to handle this situation. One is to have open places toward the end of the 40 days with congregational leaders prepared to take those times if they are not signed for. The other would be to openly ask for more than one person to take each meal slot. This can pay extra benefits if those fasting at the same time might be able to meet for their prayer time.

Sometimes it would be a good idea if the congregation had a

special new program or event (such as the ministry of a new pastor or a revival) which needed a prayer boost to get started. The event would follow the time of prayer and fasting, with the participants praying for the event for forty days. It would also give those praying a part in the new program, and they would have a greater interest in its success.

Bible reading marathons

My first experience with a Bible reading marathon was a county wide effort lead by Robbie Weathers of Elkton, KY. It was the weekend before the Presidential election of 2008 in the United States. It started on Friday evening and continued until noon on Tuesday, which was Election Day. It was outside in the city square. There was a tent nearby with the sign-up sheet, security, refreshments, and a place of fellowship where people would gather before and/or after their time reading. The reading platform was at the top of some steps going into the Old County Courthouse. There was a microphone provided.

It takes about 90-100 hours to read the Bible aloud from cover to cover. Some people read quickly and others very slowly.

I remember signing up for two readings. One was in the middle of Friday night (early Saturday morning) to get the feel of a quiet night and hearing the Word read out in the empty city. The other time I signed up was at 11:45 AM on Tuesday, which was the last reading. I wanted to read the very end of Revelation. However, at 11:45am, my portion was in the book of Hebrews. So I missed it. We have to be flexible and have some people on hand to read after the projected time in case of a miscalculation.

My second experience with a Bible reading marathon was in Belfast, Northern Ireland, in the summer of 2011. I picked the first week of summer since we would have the most daylight. We started at 10am on a Monday morning and concluded at 2pm on Friday. We got ahead of schedule so in the middle of the night we made adjustments and actually read some books twice. Belfast is a much divided city, and it was so gratifying to see over 120 people from over 40 congregations participating in our marathon. There were over 20 clergy who also read. These people were from all parts of the city and from many towns outside of Belfast. It was a cross community effort with both Catholics and Protestants reading together.

There were a couple of congregations who signed up for a 3-hour block in the evening. As one person read, the others would roam the streets and talk to people about the Lord. In fact, by the end of the marathon, 7 people gave their lives to Jesus. Here are some basic guidelines and suggestions we gave to our readers prior to their arrival.

1. You can use whatever translation is most comfortable for you. Bring your Bible, you know it best.

2. Please arrive about 10 minutes ahead of your scheduled time. This will allow you to see where the previous reader is in the Bible, and you can look over the section you will be reading.

3. The easiest transition would be for the previous reader to finish a chapter and then you would take over in a new chapter. You would then do the same. This would likely mean you would start and finish a few minutes before or after your scheduled time. This is not always possible as some chapters would go on for a long time. In those cases, we would hope to find the end of a paragraph.

4. Generally speaking, the new reader should stand next to the current reader. The outgoing reader will then find a suitable place for a transition.

5. All readers are encouraged to arrive early and stay late. The more people gathered around the better; especially if people stop in to inquire about what we are doing.

6. If (I should say when) you come to a word you may not know exactly how to pronounce, just do the best you can, mumble perhaps, but move on quickly. You may skip verses if they contain

lots of difficult names. You may want to summarize the verse quickly and move on. Such as in Acts 2, when people from many lands are hearing those at Pentecost speaking their language. It would be okay to say something like "many people heard them in their own language"

7. Smile lots and have fun. We are going to proclaim light and love. And thank you for being a part of this great adventure.

Rather than have the readers standing inside the sanctuary at the pulpit or lectern, it would be best for the Bible reading marathon to be visible to the community. The readers should stand at the door or just inside the front door.

Final thoughts

In World War Two, both the Nazi's and the British bombed each other unmercifully. Each was expecting the destruction to break the will of the people to continue the war. Neither side succeeded because long range bombing alone does not bring victory. As the Body of Christ engages in strategic spiritual warfare, we should not expect the devil and his hoard of demons to run away in fear. We can expect a cunning counter attack. They will do everything to keep us from not carrying a cross, reading the Bible, having a prayer vigil, or engaging in any or all of the strategic spiritual warfare tactics described in this book. It is vital to remain steadfast and aware of our spiritual surroundings at all times.

Over 50,000 British airmen died in the total bombing campaign of the war. So, the idea that Strategic operations are operating in a safe place behind the lines is not true. Just as the actions of brave men far away from the front lines have made a difference in conflicts, such as the Second World War, the actions of Christians in strategic spiritual warfare will make a difference in the Kingdom of God. Every Christian can participate in strategic spiritual warfare.

Look how the battle at the front lines was determined by

what happened elsewhere and at previous times. The result of the submarine battles on the sea determined the amount of beans and bullets available on the front lines. Going further, it was the success of the code breakers of Bletchley Park, which gave the advantages to the Allies in the submarine war. In 1944, the war production in the United States and the Soviet Union was on the increase. In Germany, war production was on the decrease. This was due in part to the Allied bombing of Nazi war factories, and the Allies ability to protect the factories in the United States from planned Nazi raids. War production, bombing raids, and intercepting enemy codes are three other strategic war battles.

There is a cycle in strategic war in which one area can determine the success in other places. Intercepting enemy communication can lead to successful attacks on submarines, which allows for the increased war production to reach the front line.

In the same way a successful 40 days of prayer and fasting in a congregation can bring a heightened awareness and desire for the Bible, which could in turn bring a deeper dedication to intercessory prayer. Each weapon of our warfare will strengthen the other weapons, bringing a presence of the Kingdom of Heaven into a community.

As we come to the end of this book, I do not want to impress upon the reader that this is the end of the list of weapons of strategic spiritual warfare, nor an exhaustive study of how the weapons listed can be utilized to bring glory to Our Lord Jesus. In many ways the weapons of our warfare seem difficult to organize since they work in so many interchangeable ways. A look at any one weapon results in an appreciation for the effectiveness of many other weapons. Just as a heavy-duty machine gun and a light weight rifle are used together in combat, carrying the cross and proclaiming the Word can work together in strategic spiritual warfare.

We know light always conquers the darkness. Have you ever been in a lighted hallway and opened a door into a dark room? Has the darkness ever come out into the hallway making the hallway dark? No, never. The light always enters the darkness.

Jesus is the light of the world, and the Church is the light of the world. We will always conquer darkness. The key to victory is to bring the light of Jesus Christ into the darkness of the world, and using the weapons discussed in this book can make this a reality.

It is my prayer that each reader will be stimulated to seek out more knowledge of new weapons, and new methods of using our divinely powerful weapons, to rain down havoc on the powers of darkness surrounding us. May Jesus Christ demonstrate His mercy, love, and power, to fulfill His purposes, and build His Kingdom, "on earth as it is in Heaven."

You can contact the author by emailing

strategicspiritualwarfare@yahoo.com

At **Maurice Wylie Media**, we collaborate with ministries, businesses and author's through branding, publishing, branded websites and P.R. Why don't you contact us to see how we can help you!

Visit

www.MauriceWylieMedia.com

sales@mauricewyliemedia.com

Lightning Source UK Ltd.
Milton Keynes UK
UKOW01f0939180717
305535UK00001B/42/P